Machiavelli's
The Prince

READER'S GUIDES

Bloomsbury *Reader's Guides* are clear, concise, and accessible introductions to key texts in literature and philosophy. Each book explores the themes, context, criticism, and influence of key works, providing a practical introduction to close reading, guiding students toward a thorough understanding of the text. They provide an essential, up-to-date resource, ideal for undergraduate students.

Reader's Guides available from Bloomsbury:

Aristotle's *Metaphysics*, Edward Halper
Aristotle's *Politics*, Judith A. Swanson and C. David Corbin
Badiou's *Being and Event*, Christopher Norris
Berkeley's *Principles of Human Knowledge*, Alasdair Richmond
Berkeley's *Three Dialogues*, Aaron Garrett
Deleuze and Guattari's *What is Philosophy?*, Rex Butler
Deleuze's *Difference and Repetition*, Joe Hughes
Derrida's *Writing and Difference*, Sarah Wood
Hegel's *Phenomenology of Spirit*, Stephen Houlgate
Heidegger's *Later Writings*, Lee Braver
Hume's *Enquiry Concerning Human Understanding*, Alan Bailey and Dan O'Brien
Kant's *Critique of Aesthetic Judgement*, Fiona Hughes
Kierkegaard's *Fear and Trembling*, Clare Carlisle
Kuhn's *The Structure of Scientific Revolutions*, John Preston
Locke's *Essay Concerning Human Understanding*, William Uzgalis
Machiavelli's *The Prince*, Miguel Vatter
Mill's *Utilitarianism*, Henry R. West
Nietzsche's *Beyond Good and Evil*, Christa Davis Acampora and Keith Ansell Pearson
Nietzsche's *The Birth of Tragedy*, Douglas Burnham and Martin Jesinghausen
Nietzsche's *Thus Spoke Zarathustra*, Clancy Martin and Daw-Nay Evans
Plato's *Republic*, Luke Purshouse
Plato's *Symposium*, Thomas L. Cooksey
Rawls's *A Theory of Justice*, Frank Lovett
Sartre's *Being and Nothingness*, Sebastian Gardner
Schopenhauer's *The World as Will and Representation*, Robert L. Wicks
Wittgenstein's *Philosophical Investigations*, Arif Ahmed

A Reader's Guide

Machiavelli's
The Prince

MIGUEL VATTER

B L O O M S B U R Y
LONDON • NEW DELHI • NEW YORK • SYDNEY

Bloomsbury Academic

An imprint of Bloomsbury Publishing Plc

50 Bedford Square	1385 Broadway
London	New York
WC1B 3DP	NY 10018
UK	USA

www.bloomsbury.com

Bloomsbury is a registered trade mark of Bloomsbury Publishing Plc

First published 2013

British Library Cataloguing in Publication Data
A catalogue record for this book is available from the British Library.

ISBN: HB: 978–0–8264–9876–2
PB: 978–0–8264–9877–9
ePub: 978–1–4411–7602–8
ePDF: 978–1–4411–6497–1

Library of Congress Cataloging-in-Publication Data
Vatter, Miguel E.
Machiavelli's the prince : a reader's guide / Miguel Vatter.
pages cm.
Includes bibliographical references and index.
ISBN 978-0-8264-9877-9 (pbk.)– ISBN 978-0-8264-9876-2 (hardcover)–
ISBN 978-1-4411-7602-8 (ebook (epub))
– ISBN 978-1-4411-6497-1 (ebook (pdf)) 1. Machiavelli, Niccol?, 1469-1527.
Principe. 2. Political science–Philosophy. 3. Political ethics. I. Title.
JC143.M3946V38 2013
320.1–dc23
2013015421

Typeset by Fakenham Prepress Solutions, Fakenham, Norfolk NR21 8NN
Printed and bound in India

CONTENTS

ACKNOWLEDGMENTS

This little volume comes more than ten years after my first attempt to write about Machiavelli in a far longer book. At the time, I had exhausted my ideas on the subject and was fairly sure I would never return to it. If I have now decided to repeat myself it is because I see some things differently, and I owe this in great part to the stimulus provided by other scholars, from whose works and conversation I have learnt a great deal since my first go at Machiavelli, and in particular Jérèmie Barthas, Roberto Esposito, Marco Geuna, Filippo del Lucchese, Victoria Kahn, John McCormick, Cary J. Nederman, Miguel Saralegui, and Quentin Skinner. I owe a special debt of gratitude to Vasileios Syros, who introduced me to a vast range of literature of which I had been entirely unaware, and especially for taking the trouble to read and comment on the entire manuscript of this book. All remaining mistakes are mine. I wish to thank Ben Stork for his work in editing the manuscript. Lastly, I am grateful to my family: to Vanessa Lemm for her support of my writing despite having far weightier academic responsibilities of her own, and to our children Lou, Esteban, and Alizé, for showing patience toward their father when he spends too much time at his desk.

ABBREVIATIONS

Citations will be to book and chapter, followed by page number. Unless followed by an abbreviation, all citations refer to *The Prince*, translated and edited by W. J. Connell, Boston: Bedford/St. Martin's, 2005.

Other citations from the works of Machiavelli are indicated by the following abbreviations:

D   *Discourses on Livy*, translated by H. C. Mansfield and N. Tarcov, Chicago: University of Chicago Press, 1996.

HF   *History of Florence*, translated by L. Banfield and H. C. Mansfield, Princeton: Princeton University Press, 1988.

For other works by Machiavelli mentioned in this book, I refer to their English translation in:

CW   *Machiavelli: The Chief Works and Others*, 3 vols, translated and edited by A. Gilbert, Durham: Duke University Press, 1965.

For the Italian edition of *The Prince* I have used:

Niccolò Machiavelli, *Il Principe*, edited by G. Inglese, Turin: Einaudi, 1995.

For the Italian edition of Machiavelli's works I have used:

O   Niccolò Machiavelli, *Opere*, 3 vols., edited by C. Vivanti, Turin: Einaudi, 1999.

CHAPTER ONE

Context

The Renaissance and the Machiavellian "moment"

The life of a political historian

Niccolò Machiavelli is one of the finest plants to have grown in the extraordinarily fertile soil of Renaissance Florence, the city where he was born on May 3, 1469, and died on June 22, 1527. Like many of the other great artists, thinkers, and statesmen of his time, Machiavelli did not come from one of the wealthy and noble families that ran the affairs of the cities. But his father, Bernardo, a lawyer and an amateur intellectual (or "humanist" as they called themselves), tried, within his modest means, to provide his son with a respectable "liberal arts" education, despite not being able to afford the schooling necessary to teach at a university or practice law. Unless you were born with the proverbial silver spoon, the only avenues to ascend the rungs of Florentine society consisted in developing an ability for trading and banking (which required an education in the rudiments of mathematics and bookkeeping as well as in writing letters to clients and associates) or in acquiring some knowledge in the newly re-established disciplines of the "humanities." Study of the humanities required an education in Latin, perhaps even Greek, in order to profit from the classical culture of the Romans and Greeks (their rhetoric, histories, and politics). Such a "liberal" education had become an essential requisite for anyone wishing to participate in governing the free cities of Italy since their rise in the twelfth and thirteenth centuries.

Bernardo Machiavelli must have been a relatively respected figure in Florentine humanist circles since he was featured in a dialogue *On Laws and Legal Judgments* written by the well-known humanist and Platonist, former chancellor of Florence, Bartolomeo Scala. Machiavelli's passion for politics and for the humanities was therefore inculcated in him by his father since early on. At the time, the idea of a public library was just beginning to reappear in Italy after centuries of utter neglect, and the humanists started a craze for books that remains to our days unabated. To possess a well-stocked library, possibly with copies of recovered ancient manuscripts, was therefore a sign of prestige. Given his modest means, Bernardo did his best to accumulate a respectable library, from which Machiavelli acquainted himself with some Greek and Roman historians and philosophers (Livy and Cicero, Polybius and Aristotle among others), some Scholastic philosophy (Aquinas), and some Italian poetry and literature (Dante, Petrarch, Boccaccio among others).

Machiavelli's overriding passion was not the contemplative life but politics, the active life. In comparison with other humanists of his age, he was not erudite and lacked the antiquarian's love of ancient books for their own sake: he read and wrote whatever he thought useful in making sense of the political world where he carried on his diplomatic career. Only once he had lost his office and found himself unemployed and disgraced could he afford to spend his evenings reading and thinking in the company of ancient writers "where, received lovingly by them, I eat the only food which is mine, and for which I was born." But even such study had the purpose of writing works intended to attract the attention of those currently in power or those who could one day climb to power: anyone who could help bring him back into the active world of politics. In any case, as he put it with inimitable self-deprecating wit, even while jobless and in exile, attention to books had to wait until he had "loafed about the whole day, playing *cricca* and backgammon," in a nearby inn with "a butcher, a miller and two brickmakers ... in this way, folded up with this lice, I shake the mold from my brain" (Letter to Vettori, December 10, 1513, p.139).

His extensive writings, which began in the form of reports and notes composed while in the business of a political career, were from the start a mixture of things learned "through long experience of modern things and constant readings about ancient things" (Dedication, p.40). But it was not this particular mix of ancient and modern that made his thoughts so special, for the same could be said of the writings of previous humanist chancellors and other policymakers. Unique for his time was the fact that Machiavelli brought together modern historical experience and classical political intelligence in order to fashion an understanding of politics from the point of view of the people and not of the nobility: through Machiavelli, the aristocratic political insights of the ancients were brought into contact with the material world of those modest individuals with whom he drank, played cards, and swore during his daytime loafing. He wrote plays for them, while his histories painted them back on the stage of history, from which they had been excluded since ancient times.

Machiavelli's life coincided with Florence's golden age, as—along with the other great Italian republic, Venice—it became the jewel of the Italian Renaissance, and the reason why it is still visited and admired today by millions. Florence at the time prospered primarily from its commercial and banking activities.[1] Like Athens at its highest point, which according to Thucydides was a democracy in name only but in effect was led by one man alone (Pericles), Florence, nominally a republic in the hundred of years prior to Machiavelli's birth, was in reality dominated by a few noble families, highest among them the "fatal" family of the Medici. They viewed Florence as the new Athens and for that reason leveraged their considerable resources to generate an enormous amount of "cultural capital," which was the foundation of their power: they spun an extremely complicated but effective web of political clientele, of favors given and received with other noble families, assuring them that, whatever government might be in place, they pulled its strings from their palaces. But their cultural capital also, and crucially, consisted in the patronage of humanists, artists, and philosophers who, like well-orchestrated puppets, came on the public stage of Florence to play out the comedy of democracy to distract from the tragedy of oligarchy. Machiavelli was the first Florentine intellectual to laugh at this spectacle and draw the curtain back on the tragedy, thereby writing the "effective truth" about political life. He did so through his political treatises, in his theatrical dramas, and lastly in a revolutionary history of Florence.

Although Florence was wealthy, beautiful, and "wise" thanks to the enlightened despotism exercised by Cosimo de' Medici, the "father of the country," and his son Lorenzo the Magnificent, it was also politically weak in comparison with the real powers of the time in Italy. These powers were, in a literal and figural sense, foreign powers. They included the emergent monarchies of Spain and France to the west, and England to the north; the Swiss republics and the German Emperor on the other side of the Alps; and the Saracen Empire to the East. Italy was hopelessly divided into a myriad of nominally independent city-states which, in reality, were constantly gobbled up and spat out by the strongest cities and principalities: in the first place Rome as the seat of the Catholic Church and its surrounding Papal states, the Kingdoms of Naples and Sicily, the Duchy of Milan, and the Republic of Venice. All of them had more power than Florence, and all of them kept one eye on their internal rivals and the other eye on capturing the favor or avoiding the enmity of the external powers. Florence could make a claim that, culturally speaking, it spoke for the Italian "nation," but politically, as a nation state, Italy did not exist, and Florence was both too weak to produce Italian unity and, under the regime of the Medici, too focused on currying favors with the foreign monarchies in order to make such an attempt.

In 1494, when Machiavelli was 25 years old, everything changed: the tenuous balance between existing Italian powers was shattered when the French king, Charles VIII, invaded Italy, set on getting for himself the kingdom of Naples. The French armies met risible resistance in their advance into Italy, and entered Florence without having to use any violence. Piero, the son of Lorenzo il Magnifico, who had taken over the government at his father's death, even allowed the French to mark with chalk which palaces of the wealthy and noble families would house the king's court and generals. To further ingratiate himself with the French king, Piero also gave Charles VIII parts of the dominions held by Florence with its fortresses. Revealing to the world its impotence, Florence lost control of its main subject city, Pisa. The Medici regime proved itself incapable of sparing Florence this humiliation, and the people of Florence revolted against it, siding with one of the most singular characters to emerge out of the Renaissance, the Dominican friar Girolamo Savonarola.[2]

Savonarola was one of many "heretics" that sprung up, in worrisome numbers if considered from the Pope's perspective, throughout Western Christendom in the hundred years prior to Machiavelli's birth. These "heretics" were scandalized by the moral corruption of the Popes and their courts, which they chastised publicly. Although at times they managed to gain considerable support among the poor, for the most part the feudal lords, princes, and emperors ignored them and refused them the protection of their arms. Lacking protection, they often ended up in jail or at the stake. All this changed quite abruptly when one of these heretics, Machiavelli's contemporary, Luther, succeeded in inciting a revolution against the Church, setting off the Reformation, whose long shock waves marked the beginning of the end of the hegemony of kings and popes in Europe. None the less, the harsh lessons of persecution impressed upon "heretics" the importance of being politically savvy when taking on the Church, and Savonarola was certainly among the most savvy of all heretics prior to Luther.

Savonarola had begun preaching to wild success in Florence a few years before the French invasion, prophesying that the city was doomed by the corrupt ways of the Medici. Even the "Athenian" philosophers patronized by the Medici, above all Ficino and Pico della Mirandola, were seduced by Savonarola's speeches, if not by his ideas; even Athens could do little against the resurgence of Jerusalem. The Medici and the other noble families grew timorous of his prophetic rhetoric, which proved hypnotic not only to the masses, but to the privileged sons and daughters of these families.[3]

Savonarola's political project was the opposite of the Medici's: he proposed to turn Florence not into the new Athens that it had been with Cosimo and Lorenzo, but into a new Jerusalem, God's kingdom on earth, with Christ as its head and the Florentine people, represented by a *Consiglio Grande* or large parliament, as its body. It was Savonarola, this messianic preacher of the renovation of Christianity and the destruction of Roman corruption, this foretaste of the Reformation, who was responsible for instituting the Florentine Republic after the expulsion of Piero de' Medici. It was Savonarola's Republic that gave Machiavelli his first real break, granting him access to the world of political affairs that the Florentine oligarchs would never have conceded him. Although Machiavelli remained incredulous with respect to Savonarola's prophecies, he learnt from the friar never to underestimate the importance of other-worldly religion for the conduct of worldly affairs. He would repay Savonarola with much attention in his later writings, and in many ways rescue his posthumous fame from the accusations of the Church. The birth of the Florentine Republic did not occur at a propitious moment. The new government was thrown into a dizzying maelstrom of changing political allegiances and conspiracies, where those who seemed friends of the city one day were its bitter foes the next, and vice versa. The Republic's new government lacked entirely the know-how, the courage, and especially the daring required to establish itself in Italy as the Roman Republic had once done (despite Florentine civic pride in having been founded as a Roman colony in Etruscan territory, and Florentine humanists' penchant for speaking as if Roman blood coursed their veins). Thus, when Pope Alexander VI, father of Cesare Borgia, persecuted Savonarola on the grounds of heresy and demanded that the Florentine Republic hand him over, the Republican government "resisted" the Pope and refused to send their founder to Rome. Instead, they chose to hang him from the government palace themselves, before burning his body in the main square of the city. Ficino, the court philosopher of the Medici, even went so far as to identify him as the Antichrist. Machiavelli would later draw an important lesson from this fate of "unarmed" prophets.

A few days after Savonarola's execution, for reasons that remain unclear but may have to do with his father's friendship to Scala, the ex-chancellor, or perhaps to a less than friendly report on Savonarola's preaching he wrote for the Florentine ambassador to Rome, Machiavelli was appointed a secretary on foreign policy to the committee of magistrates charged with decisions on war and peace in the new Republic. He remained at this high diplomatic post for 14 years, until the fall of the Republic in 1512.

Although France had humiliated Florence, the Republic saw no better way to fend off its Italian enemies than by courting the aid of the French king in order to maintain control over its dominions in Tuscany, including several rebellious smaller city-states not used to living under another city's control. Machiavelli's job consisted in helping fashion a diplomatic course that would quell these rebellions and, above all, find a way to regain control over Pisa, which became the veritable obsession of Florentine foreign policy during this republican period. The requirements of Florentine foreign policy sent Machiavelli on many diplomatic missions to France, central Italy, and Rome. There he came within sight and, at times, speaking distance of some of the major political and artistic personalities of his time, who later peopled his theoretical writings: the King of France, the Holy Roman Emperor, a couple of Popes, several Italian princes, princelings, and tyrants, and artists like Leonardo da Vinci. His encounters and dealings with these characters are well documented by the diplomatic briefs and reports he sent back to Florence as well as by the little essays he composed based on his foreign policy experiences. This cache of material makes up the incubation chamber of his political thought.

Among his "long experience of modern things," surely the most significant one consisted in his coming to know the power of the great new monarchies: first the French monarchy, then the German empire. His longest writings while in office are essays recounting his experiences with these monarchies, trying to decode the roots of their power as much as their hidden weaknesses (the latter being the kind of knowledge most useful to the Florentine Republic). His first diplomatic mission to the French court was an embarrassing affair. The Florentines promised to pay the French in exchange for military support in order to re-conquer Pisa. When these attempts came to a miserable failure in part due to the reliance on mercenary commanders and foreign armies that were uninterested in prevailing for the sake of Florentine interests, Machiavelli was sent to France to renegotiate the deal and keep Florence from having to pay for nothing. But the French king and his court knew Florence lacked any military force of its own and therefore was entirely dependent on the king's whim. The message was made known to Machiavelli in a famous exchange with the Cardinal of Rouen, which he later recounts in detail in *The Prince* as I discuss below.

Another major experience of Machiavelli's diplomatic period had to do with containing the meteoric rise of Pope Alexander VI's son, Cesare Borgia. Faithful to his Roman namesake, Cesare was hell-bent on consolidating the Papal dominions and conquering as much Tuscan territory as Florence would let him have, in order to carve out a chunk of central Italy to establish a state of his own. To achieve this goal, Cesare engaged in a daring and cruel game of political brinkmanship consisting in eliminating as many other competitors (both tyrannies and self-governed cities) as possible, while trying to "legitimate" his new state vis-à-vis its biggest neighbor, the Florentine Republic. Machiavelli was sent by the new Republic to play a game of cat and mouse with Cesare, the new prince, which consisted of testing the other's friendship by bluffing about who had the backing of the decisive kingmaker, the French monarch. Although Machiavelli was outwitted by Cesare, he would bear the ruthless tyrant no ill will. On the contrary, not unlike he did with the memory of Savonarola, once his beloved Republic was destroyed, Machiavelli stylized Cesare's political prowess into the picture of a new ideal prince and as an inspiration for a daring new plan to reunite Italy.[4]

Cesare's veiled threats of invading Florence in one lightning strike, communicated by Machiavelli's panicky diplomatic briefs to the Florentine government, convinced the Republic that it needed to set up a more effective executive power, someone who could match the military and strategic virtuosity of a Caesar for the sake of a Republic. In 1502 the Republic appointed Piero Soderini as a life-time "standardbearer" or president. Machiavelli became Soderini's faithful and closest advisor. From that position of confidence he had ample opportunity to see how much this honorable, honest and patriotic republican fell short of the cunning, cruelty, and audacity of a Cesare Borgia. As a consequence, Machiavelli witnessed how the honest politician fell into the traps set by the internal and external enemies of the Republic, until nothing of the new liberty remained.

Florence's experience with the French king convinced Machiavelli that money could not buy military victory unless a city taxed its wealth to create an army of its own. His chilling encounters with Cesare Borgia convinced him at the same time that worldly success depended on the happy match between political virtuosity (*virtù*) and luck (*fortuna*). This match was not made in heaven; it was not pre-determined by divine providence nor written in the stars. Political success depended on finding ways to cope with the unpredictable swerves of events which rain down on human beings outside of any providential logic or astrological necessity. Already, while in office Machiavelli did his best to spare his Republic the sad fate awaiting it. Through Soderini he was given the role he had always lobbied for, namely that of creating Florence's first people's army or militia, with the intent of taking Pisa. Florence succeeded in this enterprise in 1509, and this is perhaps Machiavelli's only political success. Strengthening the popular militia became the focus of Machiavelli's involvement in internal politics, but it cost him the enmity of the Florentine nobility, who were pressing for

Florence to drop its alliance with France and instead join the Pope and the Spanish king, all in view of regaining control of the city for themselves. Machiavelli ultimately failed in his project to build a Florentine people's army strong enough to withstand the infantries of Spain and of the Swiss, and thus scare off the Florentine aristocrats. This military failure sealed the fate of the Republic and determined his future obsession with discovering the true "art of war" in modern times.

The third and last significant political experience that Machiavelli had during his time in office took him to Rome and brought him face to face with the mysterious political "art" embodied by the Catholic Church and its Court of princes (the cardinals) and king (the Pope). For centuries, this Court ruled over a spiritual and worldly kingdom of global proportions which miraculously outlived every barbarian invasion, every heretical movement, every emperor and monarch that it confronted, without having any of the military means of its enemies. After the death of Pope Alexander VI, Cesare Borgia, in his first and last miscalculation, backed the election of another nobleman, Julius II, believing the latter's promises to support his political project. The day he was elected, Julius II reneged on this promise and put Cesare in jail. Unlike Cesare, Julius set out to conquer central Italy without a proper army, using his words rather than the sword, and succeeded where Cesare had failed, deposing ruthless tyrants without having to massacre them. How could this be? How could two entirely different approaches to gaining and holding onto power meet, one after the other, with such favor? What did these lessons teach us about the nature of politics and of history? Observing in sheer disbelief Julius's unarmed conquest, Machiavelli set down his reflections on this puzzle in a letter written to his political boss's nephew, the *Ghiribizzi al Soderino*; this letter is Machiavelli's most philosophical piece of writing prior to his post-exile "scientific" writings, already containing his intuitions concerning the relation between fortune and virtue that crown the last two chapters of *The Prince*.

In his dealings with Rome, Machiavelli had ample opportunity to study up close the essence of Papal politics, which consisted in inviting the intervention of foreign powers into Italian politics, then playing one foreign invader against another. In this cunning way, the Church ensured that no one Italian state would have the power to control the whole country and unify it, thereby leaving the Church as the ultimate arbiter not only of Italian, but also of European politics. During Machiavelli's last years in office, the Papacy first made an alliance with the French and the Spanish against Venice, dealing this Republic a bitter defeat, only to then turn around and ally itself with the Venetians, the Spanish, and the English against the French, under the battle cry to "free" Italy from their "barbarian" scourge. The Holy Alliance, led by the Spanish forces, dealt a decisive blow to the French army in Italy in 1512; the blow was doubled by the Swiss trouncing of the French army in Lombardy. These defeats repulsed France from Italy, thereby depriving the Florentine Republic of its only important ally. The Florentine Republic fell soon afterward, when its president took flight once the Cardinal Giovanni de' Medici (who shortly there-after became Pope Leo X) marched into Tuscany to reclaim his family's city, and Machiavelli's popular militia was decimated at the hands of the Spanish and Swiss infantries.

In 1513, a year into Medici control of the city, Machiavelli was implicated in an anti-Medici conspiracy; he was imprisoned and tortured. He survived the ordeal, believing one of the Medici family took pity on him, and was sent into exile to his country house outside of Florence. That same year, at the latest by 1514, he wrote the short treatise on principalities now better known as *The Prince*. He first intended to dedicate the work to the brother of the Pope, Giuliano de' Medici, with whom it appears he might have been acquainted. Probably after the death of Giuliano, Machiavelli changed the dedication to Giuliano's nephew, Lorenzo de' Medici, who in 1515 took over the leadership of Florence: the change in dedicatees proves beyond a doubt that Machiavelli was extremely anxious to get back in favor with Florence's ruling family. Although Machiavelli had had little to do with the Medici in the preceding years, after the fall of the Republic his life became heavily dependent on their favor, and this also meant winning the favor of the Papacy (since both Leo and later his cousin, Cardinal Giulio, became Popes). The dedications of *The Prince* to the Medici scions failed to secure Machiavelli entrance into the world of Medici politics and it is likely that neither recipient ever read the manuscript (which was published only after Machiavelli's death). If any of their advisors did read the book, this may even have been the reason the Medici, at first, not only ignored Machiavelli but actively dissuaded any members of the family from listening to his advice.

Machiavelli's second attempt to work himself into the graces of the Medici was therefore somewhat more subtle and indirect. He accepted an invitation, probably around 1515, to lead an informal seminar on his favorite Roman historian, Titus Livy, in the country garden of Bernardo Rucellai, a wealthy and cultivated ally of the Medici who happened to be particularly fascinated with the roots of Roman greatness. Young members of the Florentine aristocracy, the future cadres of Medici rule, attended, hoping to learn how Roman political wisdom could help the wealthy élites maintain control over Florence, just like the Roman patricians managed to keep the plebeians in abeyance for centuries.[5] It is to them, these future princes of the city, that Machiavelli later dedicated his famous book on the Roman Republic, entitled the *Discourses on Livy* (also unpublished in his lifetime), and a discussion on Roman military strategy, entitled the *Art of War*, which was the only major political work published in his lifetime. Both of these were the products of these conferences.

No one knows exactly what Machiavelli said in his informal lessons, but we do know that some of the aristocrats in his audience, perhaps seduced by the mixed messages regarding the virtues of the plebeians contained in Machiavelli's lectures, were later accused of conspiring to eliminate the Medici and set up a new Republic in Florence. These democratically inclined aristocrats were discovered and killed. Machiavelli narrowly escaped persecution a second time, probably because his open attempts to gain favor with the Medici and their aristocratic supporters were beginning to look convincing.

Be that as it may, a year or so later Machiavelli composed a theatrical hit, the *Mandragola*, which assured him a good measure of fame and a better fortune. The racy comedy tells the story of an older man, unable to have children with his much younger and beautiful wife, Lucrezia (Bernardo Rucellai, unable to make the political wisdom of the Romans bear fruit for him?). Lucrezia was desired by a far younger and good-looking admirer, Callimaco (the young aristocrats and republican conspirators?), who is advised by an unscrupulous marriage counselor, Ligurio (Machiavelli, the teacher of politics?), to mask himself as a doctor and convince the old man that his wife should drink a magical potion of mandrake

(Machiavelli's new interpretation of Roman history?) in order to enhance her fertility prior to their having intercourse again. The young doctor warns the old man that the potion has an unpleasant side-effect: it causes the death of whoever first has sex with his wife. Thus the old man is convinced to send an unwary fool into his wife's bedroom to at once defile their marriage and pay the ultimate price for it. He then asks a priest, Timoteo, to convince his pious wife that although adultery is a mortal sin, there are certain special circumstances in which it is licit to sin for the sake of a higher good. The comedy ends with the wife rather enjoying the attentions of the young man during their first night, and deciding to take him on as her permanent lover.

Funny stories of lascivious and unscrupulous priests scandalized no one in the Renaissance, least of all the members of the Pope's court, and Machiavelli's suggestions in *The Art of War* to the Florentine nobility with regard to making their armies more formidable were gratefully accepted. So it is not surprising that in 1520 Machiavelli was asked by Cardinal Giulio to offer suggestions for a new constitution that the Medici wanted to give Florence. Faithful to his dual nature of theorist of republican power and advisor to new princes, Machiavelli's proposed solution was typically overdetermined. In his *Discourse on Remodeling the Government of Florence* he suggested that the Medici should establish a Republic in Florence in which a Constitution would give a portion of power to the people and the rest to the noble families. At the same time, he also counseled that the Pope and the Cardinal, both Medici, should retain full control over this constitutional arrangement by having unlimited power of appointing the government, until their deaths. Thereafter, the Florentines having learnt the advantages of this mixed arrangement, the Constitution should be allowed to work its effects on its own, without any "overseer." Machiavelli thus took a central belief of neo-Roman republican constitutionalism, that good constitutions establish a mixed regime, and fused it with the neo-Platonist suggestion that every constitution ought to defer to the decisions of a wise ruler, whenever such an individual exists.

Machiavelli's suggestion to the nobility that they would be wise to share power with the people was not taken up, but he finally made it into the magical circle of Medici patronage. He received the commission from Cardinal Giulio de' Medici, who would become Pope Clement VII in 1523, for his last important piece of theoretical writing, the *History of Florence*. The Medici Pope wanted Machiavelli to write a history of his family's glorious governing of Florence in the past and up to his own days. For Machiavelli, who had experienced first-hand the dark side of Medici power, this task posed a great challenge, and he later admitted that, in order to write such a *History*, he was forced to express his own opinions in the voice of those characters who were explicitly condemned in the text.[6]

His political life ended as it had begun, with Machiavelli being assigned minor diplomatic and military missions by the Papacy on behalf of Florence, particularly those designed to ward off the threat of a foreign invasion. But this time around, Machiavelli found himself on the side of the Medici, the Papacy and the French, fighting against the army of Charles V, who was both King of Spain and Holy Roman Emperor. Once again, the king and emperor spared Florence. Rome, though, was ransacked by the Spanish, and the Medici Pope was imprisoned. The anti-Medici party in Florence grasped the opportunity to establish a Republic. Tainted by his dealings with the Medici, no one from the new government came around to offer him employment. He died shortly thereafter.

The education of a political teacher

What we call the Italian Renaissance is one of those events, few and far between, that completely revolutionized traditional ways of understanding the world and brought about a new model of "civilization." In the course of time, we have come to understand that this new civilization ushered in the "modern age" in which we still live. Machiavelli belongs to the revolutionary spirit of the Renaissance because he turned on its head the traditional under-standing of politics. The word "revolution" literally refers to a movement in which things "return to beginnings." This return is both a return to a forgotten past and a moment of renewal opening on to an unknown future. Renaissance: this means the re-birth of the ancients and the emergence of the modern. Machiavelli is a man of the Renaissance because he innovated; but he is also a man of the Renaissance because he recovered and revived the knowledge of politics once possessed by the Romans and the Greeks, which had been lost for centuries. Indeed, if it was true that, as the Church taught, Jesus Christ showed that the world is governed according to a divine plan and to divine justice, and not, despite appearances to the contrary, by chance and through violence, then what was the point of all that old knowledge, written by and for peoples ignorant of the glad tidings brought by the Savior?

The Christian vision of history was starting to crumble by Machiavelli's time. The Church itself, after a couple of hundred years of anxious waiting, started to think the Savior might take longer than expected to return and redeem human history. Theologians began to reconsider their rejection of ancient paganism: maybe some useful things could still be learnt about worldly politics from Plato, Aristotle, and Cicero, especially when they endorsed moral leaders seeking the common good of their subjects, so long as their teachings did not evidently contradict the Bible. The more secularly-minded Italian states of the late Middle Ages came to similar conclusions, and a consensus arose that the best politicians are those familiar with ancient culture. Thus, in the century prior to Machiavelli, many Florentine Chancellors were also great humanists, and knowledge of Latin was required at the higher echelons of government. More subtly, the Medici used the Platonic conceit that behind any system of law there stands always a wise man overseeing its proper functioning in order to legitimate their shadow rule over Florence.[7]

For all these reasons the question of Machiavelli's own culture is particularly important. If Machiavelli is the founder of a new way of thinking about politics, of a new political science, then the question of what he knew, of what he could have read and what he could not have known, is very significant and helps shed light on his writings; above all the relationship between history, rhetoric, philosophy, and political science are at stake here. What kind of a cultural revolution makes possible a revolution in politics? Or, as Marx said, who educates the educators?

By the time Machiavelli was starting to study Latin and began reading in his father's library, both Cicero and Aristotle—the philosophical giants who had decisively molded medieval Christian political thinking—had been newly processed by Italian humanist culture. The Italian humanists began using Cicero and Aristotle to make sense of the relatively new belief that human freedom in this world depends neither on the destiny of the Christian Church nor on that of the Christian Empire. Church and Empire were supranational and suprahistorical medieval constructions which for centuries had been sparring for pre-eminence. The great Florentine poet, Dante, as well as the great Paduan philosopher, Marsilius, attacked the traditional division of labor, according to which the Church retained the power of the keys to open Heaven while the Empire wielded the sword of peace. They defended the idea that only a human legislator or emperor could bring true peace on earth, if only he were given both the power of the keys and the power of the sword. Many today identify this defense of Empire against Church as the new dawn of Western "secularism."[8]

Be that as it may, Italian humanist culture began to see the destiny of human freedom not in the overarching unity of Church and Empire, which characterizes the *respublica Christiana* of the Middle Ages, but as intimately tied up with the independence of one's political community, city or kingdom.[9] Neither Church history nor the history of the Empire could help in understanding this experience of civic freedom, so it was natural for humanists to turn to those classical thinkers who already described it: Cicero for the Romans and Aristotle for the Greeks. We can see this typical humanist use of Cicero and Aristotle reflected in the praise of Venice, considered before Machiavelli to be the best form of republic, penned by Poggio Bracciolini, arch-famous humanist, secretary to Popes, and Florentine chancellor: "As Aristotle says, there are various sorts of constitution, of which two in particular stand out from the rest, namely monarchy and aristocracy, or what we call government by the best. Indeed, Cicero says in *De Legibus* that the best sort of constitution is that in which the best men, as he chooses to call them, are in power; men motivated by desire for praise and esteem, who keep their fatherland safe, true lovers of the republic. Such a constitution, I can say with confidence, has only ever been found in Venice. With the Venetians, only the best govern the state, under constraint of the laws, and intent, everyone of them, on the advantage of the commonwealth without consideration of personal gain."[10] Machiavelli himself believed none of this talk: he knew aristocrats had other motivations. What mattered to him was that Poggio had translated some of the earliest Greek treatises on princes by Xenophon, a disciple of Socrates, and that he had discovered the long-lost manuscript of Lucretius's poem on nature; both these books turned out to be fundamental for Machiavelli's secret education.[11]

Along with Venice, the other exemplar of civic liberty was Florence, whose origins Florentine humanists and historians liked to draw back to the Roman Republic. The liberty of Florence was praised by an entire generation of humanists, the most famous one being another chancellor of the city under the Medici, Leonardo Bruni. For these humanists, what it means for a city to be free was something that had to be relearned by studying Cicero's account of the Roman republic and political life, as well as from Roman historians like Sallust and Tacitus and their accounts of lost Roman liberty once the Republic became a principality and an Empire, thereby depriving most Roman citizens of the possibility of leading an active life, reducing them to the possession of abstract rights over life and property. Likewise, Aristotle—whose *Politics* was translated by Bruni again into Latin—taught that the highest good for a human being is a political life, and that the contemplative life is accessible only to the very few and these were more divine than human individuals. Here is Bruni's distillation of this classical political wisdom: "We do not tremble beneath the rule of one man who would lord it over us, nor are we slaves to the rule of a few. Our liberty is equal for all, is limited only by the laws, and is free from fear of men. The hope of attaining office and of raising oneself up is the same for all, provided only one put in effort and have talent and a sound and serious way of life."[12] Again, Machiavelli unmasked this nice rhetoric as pure ideology: he was all too aware of how much energy the nobility spent in keeping the common people out of power in Florence, but he did hold on to Bruni's general idea that only republics could be legitimate governments.

By Machiavelli's time, Aristotle's *Politics* was translated into Latin twice in the West: first by Moerbeke, in order to serve the Church; then by Bruni, in order to serve the city-state governed by élites. Moerbeke's translation lent ammunition to perhaps the greatest medieval rebellion to the authority of the Church in human affairs, namely, Marsilius of Padua's *Defensor Pacis* and its rejection of the idea that the Church had any legislative power. But Bruni's translation achieved another goal, namely, that of disqualifying monarchy from being the best regime, and rehabilitating the popular republic. In general, one can say that the late medieval reception of Cicero and Aristotle taught that it was necessary to return politics to its root in humanity and away from divinely revealed legislation, and in so doing made possible what we now call "civic humanism." This way of looking at politics makes up the "republican" education of Machiavelli.

From his father's library, Machiavelli would have also gathered some knowledge of the greatest Christian philosopher of the Middle Ages, Saint Thomas Aquinas, and his republican continuator, Ptolemy of Lucca. Since his father was a doctor of law, Machiavelli was familiar with the works and ideas of the medieval commentators of Roman law and canon law, which today we know as the bases for the theory of sovereignty. After all, his father is featured in Bartolomeo Scala's *Dialogue on Laws and Legal Judgments* where a discussion takes place between Bernardo and Bartolomeo centered on the legal dispute of two of the most important Italian jurists of the fourteenth century, Baldus and Bartolus, on the essence of Roman law. Thus Machiavelli was more than aware of the legalistic mentality that characterized all medieval political thought and he would have understood immediately its obvious limits: medieval legal thinking was characterized by an inability to develop a proper theory of state sovereignty. Medieval commentators spoke eloquently against tyranny but they could not explain the flood of tyrants that overwhelmed Italy and led to the crisis of civic humanism and municipal self-government.

The third element of Machiavelli's formal education consisted of those treatises written in the century preceding his youth in which humanists tried to portray a "mirror" of the legitimate prince for the up and coming despots and tyrants of Italy. The two most important classical sources for this genre were Xenophon's *The Education of Cyrus*, translated into Latin once again by Poggio, and Seneca's *On Clemency*, which popularized the Roman idea of the prince or emperor.[13] It was against this literature that Machiavelli would write *The Prince*, the book that broke for ever the "mirror, mirror" of the prince.

But had Machiavelli persevered on this path and perhaps received the full benefits of an education as a lawyer or a humanist he would not have become who he is: a thinker entirely possessed by the self-consciousness that he was opening a new path in politics. As a true man of the Renaissance, Machiavelli was aware of the importance of self-reliance in life, and thus instinctively understood that education was not merely a process of dipping into the river of tradition and letting oneself be carried away by the authority of others, but a process of self-education, of swimming against the current, of moving to the edges of the accepted curriculum of academic studies.

What other textual encounters allowed Machiavelli to wander off the beaten paths of humanistic studies? What other books or traditions, unknown prior to the Renaissance, provided him with an alternative education and with dangerous ideas? One such book stands out: Lucretius' *On the Nature of Things*. Of all rediscovered ancient books by the humanists, Lucretius was by far the most important for Machiavelli, who would put his philosophy to an entirely new and anti-aristocratic use. In 1496 Machiavelli got hold of one or possibly two printed editions of Lucretius and transcribed the manuscript for his personal use. This took great effort on his part, indicating without a doubt that Lucretius was part of Machiavelli's self-education, outside of the canon of humanistic studies.[14]

Lucretius was a Roman poet who put into Latin verse the ideas of the Greek philosopher Epicurus. Epicurus defended the doctrine of atomism and believed that the world was entirely material, not ideal as Plato and Aristotle taught. Every thing in the universe is the product of chance encounters between atoms caused by "swerves" (*clinamen*) in their linear trajectories. The universe is eternal and periodically undergoes great explosions, Big Bangs we would call them today, that rearrange everything and give rise to contingent, yet lawful, combinations of atoms that make up the things we perceive in our world. Epicurus also taught that the gods were entirely indifferent to human affairs and human beings should neither fear them nor worship them; there was no afterlife, no heaven or hell. Lastly, Epicurus taught that pleasure was the highest good. In short, Epicureanism was as close to an anti-Christian philosophy as one could find. For this reason, Epicureanism was synonymous with atheism throughout the medieval period, and even Cicero used to say that, should Epicurus' philosophy turn out to be the truth, he would still prefer Plato over truth, because Plato at least taught that virtue and pleasure are not the same. Thus, to study Epicurus meant to set aside the most cherished notions of Cicero and Aristotle, those teachers of virtue, producing a considerable distance from civic humanism, in order to end in the proximity of atheism and libertinism, both of which were to become associated with Machiavelli's name both during his lifetime and ever since.

A second tradition that falls outside of the humanist canon but may have had an important impact on the young Machiavelli is not Epicurean but Platonic. As suggested above, the Florence ruled by Cosimo de' Medici and his family aimed at becoming a new Athens, a capital of art and culture. For that reason Cosimo patronized the so-called Platonic Academy and commissioned Ficino to pursue the ambitious project of making Latin translations of Plato's and Plotinus' complete works. In comparison to Cicero and Aristotle, whose works were widely known in the late medieval period, Plato remained pretty much unknown outside the transmission of his thought in Christian mystical philosophy, and Arabic and Jewish political philosophy; all of which offered highly Aristotelianized readings of Plato. Plato owes his real renaissance in modern Europe to his reception through Byzantium in the Venetian and the Florentine Republics.

Venice came into contact with Plato's philosophy through George of Trebizond, a Cretan, who taught Greek to Venetian humanists and translated Plato's *Laws* for them. Like Poggio Bracciolini, George also made the argument that Venice, with its rule of laws over men, was the perfect form of government because modeled on Plato's ideal of a mixed regime, as sketched in *Laws*. But this was only a later turn of events in George's bizarre life. In reality, George was no friend of Platonism. He considered Plato the secret pathway through which paganism would return to Europe and overthrow Christianity, thus leading to the final battle between the Antichrist (who would be a Platonist) and Christ, bringing history to an apocalyptic end.

The reception of Plato in Florence was undertaken under entirely different circumstances. Here it was George's arch-enemy, the Byzantine Platonic philosopher Gemisthos Plethon, who was invited by Cosimo de' Medici to lecture on Plato while in Ravenna as part of an embassy sent by the Orthodox Christian Church of Constantinople to meet with the Pope to explore how to unite both branches of Christendom in light of the threat posed by the Turkish empire. Plethon's lecture so mesmerized Cosimo that he later commissioned the translation of all of Plato's works by Ficino.

The Plato that was taught by Plethon was an anti-Aristotelian, anti-Scholastic Plato. Aristotle argued that contemplative life and active life were separate forms of life: to be a good citizen you did not need to be a good philosopher, and conversely a philosopher need not be involved in politics. Plato argued the opposite: only a good philosopher can be a true citizen, and a city must be ruled by philosophers. Someone like Thomas Aquinas receives Aristotle's teaching as follows: the Church takes over the care of the contemplative life of humanity, whereas the city takes over the care of their political life. The city can receive either a monarchic, an aristocratic, or a democratic government depending on the circumstances and the degree of education of its population. The Church, in turn, rules over the city, but indirectly. On Plato's account, on the other hand, the philosopher is called to politics in order to rule over others in person, or, if not in person, then by instituting a code of laws for the people.

This Platonic belief can very easily be translated into the idea that religion must be political if it is to succeed in governing people toward their eternal happiness, and, vice versa, politics must become religious or a religion in order to have the same effect. In either case, the comfortable demarcation between Church and "state" of medieval memory was quickly vanishing. Listening to Plethon, Cosimo might very well have thought that the Church would have to strengthen its "state" to survive, and, conversely, if the "state" was going to strengthen itself and attain independence it would need to have a new religion of its own, a civil religion mixing Platonism with Christianity. It is easy to see why Cosimo de' Medici could think that this Byzantine Plato applied perfectly to his times even as it prepared the arrival of a Savonarola as much as the Medici takeover of the Papacy. Machiavelli's witnessed both during his lifetime and they indelibly marked his thinking.

Plethon spent but a few days in Florence, but Ficino, who became the court philosopher of the Medici, took up Plethon's legacy. It became Ficino's life-work to achieve this fusion of Platonism with Christianity, or a *Platonic Theology* as he entitled his most famous book. Ficino's Plato was a theologian, and Ficino called his Platonist theology *prisca theologia*.[15] This theology claimed that behind the three great monotheisms of revealed religion lay an older religion worked out by divine men, an ancient series of philosopher-prophets. Ficino thought that this series of wise men began with Moses, then passed on to the Persian Zoroaster (Nietzsche's Zarathustra), the Egyptian Hermes Trismegistus, and the Greek

Orpheus, and from there reached the Greek pre-Socratic philosophers like Pythagoras and Lycurgus, the Spartan lawgiver, before culminating in Plato (who also thought of himself as a lawgiver). Ficino's claim was that Christianity, properly interpreted, was but a variation of this older religion, perhaps the version that could make sense of all religions and bring peace among them. In any case, this conceit of an original religion of humanity eliminated the need for religious wars, for intolerance, but also denied Christ had broken history into a past and a future, because Christ was but a disciple of Zoroaster, who taught that the world, far from having an end (even an impending end), was eternal, and that everything in the world returns, again and again. There is nothing new under the sun, as Machiavelli says in the *Discourses on Livy*.

This theological Plato, although intended to bring peace between all religions, could be construed, as Ficino did in order to develop a *pia philosophia*, as a unity between paganism and Christianity, promising to overcome the medieval distinction between rational truth and truths accessible to faith alone. But this Platonism was also a great threat to Christianity, since it signaled the impending end of its rule on earth, as the earth belonged to an eternal and infinite universe. The eternal world would live on, renewing itself periodically, just like Lucretius had said, but Christianity would not return. Lucretius and Plato: reading them in these new ways could have easily persuaded Machiavelli that the time had come to orient our earthly life—that is, our political life—to the love of the world rather than to the love of God.

The Renaissance, or the value of history for life

Once the interpretation of Christian theology as a variation of the astral theology of the ancients begins, as the Florentine philosophers did during the time of the Medici, then the "novelty" of the gospel of Jesus is relativized and made to fit within the astrological calendar of human history and its ever-recurring cycles. Christian belief in a divine calendar of salvation, marked by a linear unfolding of history centered on the decisive event of the death and resurrection of Jesus Christ, is incompatible with the circularity of history that follows from the belief in the eternity of the world and in the influence planetary circles have on future events. For this reason Savonarola chastised Ficino's obsession with astrology and magic as unbecoming of Christian faith. If one now adds to this resurgence of astral theology the subterranean influence of Lucretius' atomism, according to which events are not linked to one another by a providential plan but all order emerges out of chance and either adapts to the circumstances or perishes, then it is easy to see why Machiavelli, had he known it, would agree with Shakespeare's Hamlet that "time is out of joint" as the course of the world no longer seemed to run on fixed rails.

As we saw above, Machiavelli's life offered plenty of corroboration for the belief that one's fate is not sealed at birth: everywhere around him one saw that a social nobody could rise to become a great *signore* or lord, wealthy and surrounded by artists and intellectuals, so long as they exploited the right opportunities. The individual has no Fate, and its life is not predetermined by God or Nature. Instead, every individual is a son of chance, like Oedipus. Life is about turning one's luck around, transforming our contingency into a destiny; making oneself into who one is: life is *amor fati*, the love of fate. The Renaissance is responsible for the idea that one's life is a work of art, where one takes the raw materials given to one and through craft turn them to one's favour, giving oneself a beautiful shape. This belief goes hand in hand with the other belief of the Renaissance, namely that what we call "the state" is itself a work of art, a technical achievement, and not the name for an "ethical" or "moral" way of being together with others, as the ancients had understood it. Art or craft is a function of two things: luck, or the contingency of one's situation, and virtue, the capacity to make something out of that situation. Virtue or *virtù* signifies an artistic will, a power of creation and destruction. It was left up to Machiavelli to provide the ultimate account of the state as a work of art.

Art imitates nature: this belief was held since Aristotle and maintained by Renaissance thinkers. If it is possible to mold a world in accordance with artistic or creative will, then nature itself must be creative about its forms. Nature must be such that it creates and destroys innumerable prototypes before landing on the most adequate one for a given constellation of matter, just as an artist must produce many sketches. If everything were to be made according to a fixed purpose by a primordial and transcendent first cause, as the Aristotelian universe suggests, then only the perfect form would compose nature, or nature would amount to matter shaped by these perfect forms. On this picture of nature, there would be little space left for artistic creativity, or, better, creativity would be due to the recalcitrance of matter to accept its proper form; creativity would be the space of ugliness, not beauty. Nature would not be an evolutionary process of trial and error. In order for the claims of an artistic will, for the process of self-creation, to come about it was thus necessary to question the belief in a teleological or purposive order of the cosmos. Not purpose but chance and creativity come to the fore: not form and intellect, but matter and free will. This is the world that Lucretius made possible and that Machiavelli adapted to the study of politics.

If everything is already perfect prior to the activity of human ingenuity because it is always already known to the mind of God, then there is not much point to human curiosity and experimentation with nature itself; it is enough to read the Bible to know what God's plan has in store for us, and to read Aristotle to understand the purposes of nature, since Christian philosophers were convinced he was a mere conduit for Nature herself. From the Renaissance perspective, these two beliefs lead to an education based on self-denial and *ozio* (leisure), to use the term employed by Machiavelli. But if no overarching purpose exists in nature, then it is possible to discover the order of nature by arriving, through experimentation and ingenuity, at those rules that allow us to represent the world as having an order that we can eventually master and use to better our lot. Machiavelli witnessed first hand this aesthetic-experimental approach to nature when he met Leonardo da Vinci, while he was in the service of Cesare Borgia, and with whom he planned the considerable engineering feat of attempting to divert the course of an entire river for the military purposes of conquering besieged cities. He already saw everywhere the fruits of this new ideal of knowledge in innovations in art and architecture, made possible by the invention of linear perspective by the Florentine architect Brunelleschi: a geometrical method for reproducing the world according to its three-dimensional structure.

Just as Brunelleschi built the greatest free-standing dome structure in Florence by emulating the techniques of the Roman architects in the Pantheon, just like humanists were re-learning how to read and write by following the grammar and rhetoric of the Romans, so too, it struck Machiavelli, it was possible to learn about politics from the Romans and, above all, to imitate them in actions and not just in thought. If the Christian picture of history was wrong, if everything returns an infinite amount of times, then the Romans could be made to return once again; nothing stood in the way of the possibility of their imitation. If the Aristotelian picture of nature was mistaken, then the scope for human virtue was far greater than previously thought. The model of the political state need not be given by the Church or the Empire, for these political organizations seek to mirror on earth how things look from the perspective of the King of the universe, the Kingdom of God. The eternity of the world makes it possible to recover and imitate the virtue of the Romans today, in the present, and possibly setting history on a new course; it can itself generate that swerve which brings about an entirely new social organization. Machiavelli saw his historical present as one calling for a task, a project that would move the cultural development of a people forward: the foundation of a unified and stable Italian state (a cultural and political "nation"). Some have seen here the beginning of nationalism, in the modern sense of nation-building, of wars of independence, and so on. In Italy there was no "state"; there was political chaos and a lack of order due to invasions by northern monarchies and the incompetence of Italian princes. Hence the political problem: how to create a stable political order out of nothing and produce a foundation allowing it to persevere in time. This was the problem Machiavelli set to resolve in his treatise on principalities, which we are now in a position to begin to read.

CHAPTER TWO

Overview

The Prince as a work of rhetoric and philosophy

The Prince and the modern science of politics

During the course of the last 500 years, no book has incurred more blame for giving politics the bad reputation it continues to enjoy to our days than Machiavelli's *Prince*. According to one influential version of the history of political thought, developed in the aftermath of World War Two, Machiavelli turned politics into a technique of domination and the state into a machine designed to crush under its cogs all human freedom. *The Prince* was thought to outline new rules of political conduct, a new "science" of politics that, like all other modern social sciences, remains neutral toward the values for the sake of which its techniques of power may be employed. When U.S. President Truman decided to drop the atomic bombs on Japanese civilian populations in order for the war not to drag on, his political calculus was just as "Machiavellian" as the Japanese government had been at the start of the war with their surprise attack on Pearl Harbor.

Confronted with the barbarism of totalitarian regimes and total warfare, many thinkers went further still and drew the conclusion that modern political science in its entirety was erected on the ruins of the moral picture of politics upheld by the ancients, for whom involvement in public affairs meant a life of sacrifice in the name of the common good. Machiavelli's *Prince* was thought to have torn that picture into shreds, inaugurating the modern science of politics by substituting a technical vision of politics, where what counts is how to conquer and hold on to power over others in the most efficient way possible. By giving up on the aspiration of the ancients' political wisdom or science to find a universal moral standard that could evaluate and distinguish the best from the worst political regimes, rather than merely describe their techniques of domination, Machiavelli's *Prince* was charged with setting off a process that climaxed with the horrors of totalitarian regimes in the twentieth century, regimes whose only value seems to have been creating the purest form of domination over the human species.[16] The return of barbarism on such an unheard of scale and at the height of technological development indicated that there had been no moral progress of humanity since the ancients. For some of these critics of modernity, it was time to leave Machiavelli's modern science behind and return to the political ideals of the ancients.

Side by side with this pessimistic vision of modernity, another narrative argued that modern political science, after all, designed, constructed, and perfected a modern conception of the republic that had survived and defeated authoritarian and totalitarian regimes. In this story, Machiavelli plays an entirely different role. Machiavelli's works were assiduously read and studied by all modern republican revolutionaries, from Holland and England to the United States and France, from Spinoza and Harrington to Jefferson, Adams, Rousseau, and Sièyes; in short, by everyone who engineered these modern republican constitutions that, with any luck, are still governing us. In this second narrative the revival of ancient political wisdom also plays a fundamental role, since the modern founding fathers went back to the Greek and Roman classics of political thought in search of enlightenment. But everyone acknowledged that it was Machiavelli who had given the keys to unlock the secrets withheld by the dusty tomes. Ironically, he made ancient republicanism come to life again by appreciating the "modernity" or novelty of Greek and Roman political philosophy when compared to the backdrop of more than a thousand years of Christianity.

Unlike the critics of modernity, Machiavelli did not think that the ancients were "modern" because they already knew more and better than we do about the important things in life. Rather, for him, the possibility of reviving the past opened a space for unheard-of innovation: the renewal of the Roman republic translated into the project of building a new Rome. If Machiavelli's political science is "modern," then it is so by virtue of its belief that republics emerge and live in a time of renewal, in an event of political innovation, whereas monarchies model themselves on the eternity of the cosmic or divine order.[17]

After Machiavelli, this event of political renewal received the name of "revolution." It is perhaps the most striking characteristic of modern republican experiments that all of them, without exception, arose in and through the experience of revolution. Unlike their ancient counterparts, modern republics are born out of the experience that social order is not rooted in any "natural law" but is contingent and inherently changeable; that new orders can be the product of a collective political design; that political institutions are not given once and for all but need to have in-built capacities for self-adaptation that will make the state flexible enough to withstand radical changes of situation and fortune; in short, that revolutions are necessary for the development of human freedom. None of these intuitions were accessible to monarchies since they depend on the opposite belief that there exists one correct political order (be it divine or natural) that needs to be imitated by human beings. For modern republicans, Machiavelli was the main transmission belt into the modern age of the classical ideals of republican freedom as independence and constitutional government advocated by Aristotle and Cicero, because he gave this ancient freedom a new temporal form, that of revolution.

This alternative, more optimistic, view of Machiavelli's modernity has recently led other interpreters to argue that *The Prince* is better understood as a renewal of the ancient art of "rhetoric" rather than as the first work of modern political "science."[18] Cicero once said that laws existed so that human beings could live together without masters. Rhetoric, the art of persuasion perfected by Roman writers, is the other side of the coin: because we are free, no one has the right to coerce us to follow a given course of action; they first need to persuade us that this is the right course of action for us. On this Ciceronian view, without rhetoric there can be no republican political life. It is undoubtedly for this reason that the study of rhetoric became so important for the Italian city-states that claimed independence from Church and Empire, and the renewal of rhetoric led the way to the emergence of civic humanism discussed in the previous section, which in turn is a crucial context within which to understand *The Prince*.

But just as the ancient republican ideals of political freedom required a new temporal form, that of revolution, in order to break into modernity, so too with Machiavelli's own recovery of Roman rhetoric: it had to be placed at the service of an entirely different political content, namely, persuading the ruling élites that the common people were the source of their power. Classical political wisdom was always a matter of knowing some unpleasant "truths" about how to rule people whose ultimate justification was accessible to a few wise men but otherwise had to be kept hidden from public scrutiny (for instance, the belief that there is an order of rank in nature, that some natures are superior to others and should therefore rule over them, for the benefit of the inferior natures, etc.). In order for these "truths" to be circulated among the common people, and in this way become "political," classical philosophy devised the art of rhetoric or persuasion. For classical philosophy the apparently egalitarian structure of rhetoric (you only try to persuade someone whom you deem to be your equal) was ancillary to the hierarchical teaching of wisdom. Despite their apparent support of republican ideals, the civic humanists had not dared to change this order of priority: rhetoric remained a tool of the élites.[19]

Machiavelli was the first to subvert this order: in *The Prince* rhetoric becomes an instrument of the common people to fight against the vision of the world proposed by classical wisdom, and along with that to change the relation of power between élites and masses. Machiavelli uses rhetoric in order to open up the field of politics to the participation of a previously excluded actor, the people, and in so doing he also changes the character of the study of politics, making it possible eventually to develop an experimental scientific approach to the study of social and political institutions in which the whole is the result of the causal interaction of the elementary parts. If today so much of modern political science is a matter of sophisticated "bean counting," of analysis of parliamentary procedures and electoral results, then this is in no small measure due to this revolution in the meaning of rhetoric which took its egalitarian content and turned it around to destroy the non-egalitarian political wisdom of the ancients. Modern empirical science denied just about every claim made by ancient philosophical wisdom because it began from the democratic premise that truth had to be accessible to everyone and, more importantly, testable by everyone.

The new awareness of the dependence of political freedom on the historicity and contingency of political form, and the emergence of the people as a political actor, goes a long way to explain why rhetoric emancipated itself from ancient wisdom and its focus on eternal verities and prophetic revelations. But rhetorical analysis is not enough to account for the novelty of Machiavelli's political science. Rhetoric presupposes that speakers and hearers share the same political language or vocabulary. Machiavelli's *Prince*, though, innovates the language of politics: it is a work that constructs new concepts and it does so by using arguments. The construction of a new concept is the work of philosophy, not just of rhetoric. If rhetoric could be used by the élites to keep the people in their place (namely, outside the business of government), then Machiavelli's *Prince* shows how rhetoric can also persuade the élites to give the people a different place and role in public life. But what changes in the theory of government are required to make place for the people, what new concept of the state results from this revolution, this is properly speaking a philosophical achievement. It is in this sense that this *Reader's Guide* presents *The Prince* as a work of philosophy: the construction of the concept of state through a special and new art, the *arte dello stato*, or statecraft, which contains a political knowledge accessible to everyone and for the use of everyone. *The Prince* is the first philosophical grounding of a democratic project of modernity.[20]

The plan of the Guide

This *Reader's Guide* presents the argument of *The Prince* by grouping its 26 chapters into thematic sections. The overall argument turns on the problem of the state and its relation to the democratic aspirations of a people. Each section pursues this problem from a different philosophical concern that can be divided, somewhat roughly, into concerns of an epistemological, a social, a moral, and lastly a theologico-political kind.

In the "Dedication" to *The Prince*, Machiavelli says that he is offering a new kind of "knowledge" in his book. But what kind of knowledge is it? Is it akin to ancient practical wisdom or to modern social science? Thus, *The Prince* opens with an epistemological concern, and Chapters 3 and 4 of the *Reader's Guide* try to explain what this concern is and how Machiavelli resolves it. In his treatise on principalities, Machiavelli introduces a term that would have a famous career in the modern age: the notion of state (Italian *stato*). Machiavelli's political science is intended to elucidate the rules that apply to the establishment of a state. But rules do not apply themselves by themselves. Which rules to follow and how to follow them is dependent on context, and this can be the object of rhetorical description and redescription. The problem of rule-following is one of the points where rhetoric and science touch each other. Not surprisingly, *The Prince* follows the guiding thread of rule-following in presenting its new scientific object: what kind of thing is a "state" and whose interests it is supposed to fulfill is something that is discussed, first as a rhetorical artifact, and subsequently as an object of empirical science, where rules are hypotheses that need to be falsified or verified by experiment, by contrasting them with test cases where they can fail, or to see where and why previous rules fail and other hypotheses emerge.

After discussing the nature of the state, the argument of *The Prince* shifts to the description and theorizing of the social processes within which the state is embedded. Thus Chapters 5 and 6 of the *Reader's Guide* discuss the social theory that lies at the basis of Machiavelli's political science. In the medieval era, there was no idea of the state as we have become familiar with it. The reason for this is that medieval thinking about politics is, generally speaking, a thinking about law: if one can speak of the "state" in medieval political thought, it is always as a function of what stands under laws and has the task of applying these laws. For medieval thought, the "state" is an instrument of law, and laws are given "naturally": they are certainly not imposed by a sovereign state authority. Hence medieval political thinkers tended to believe in something called "natural law," universal precepts of morality that are common to all human beings in virtue of their rational character. For us today, things are exactly the other way around: if there were not a sovereign state that imposed, by force, certain social conditions, no one would or could guarantee that any laws would ever be applied.[21] Chaos comes before order; social conflict comes before social consensus; Machiavelli intuits this fundamental aspect of social reality, and on its basis he calls for the construction of the state. Indeed, in this part of his argument, Machiavelli explains that the construction of a modern state only makes sense on the basis of the awareness that social conflict and competition are the real engines of historical change. Because Machiavelli assigns priority to conflict over consensus, he is able to perceive the first manifestations of the separation of society and religion from the state; the rise of individualism; the emergence of free markets and capitalism—all of which are important and new realities that factor in his way of thinking about politics and that account for its "modernity."

In Chapter 7 of the *Reader's Guide* the moral concern comes to the fore: *The Prince* shifts to a discussion of the person who is charged with matters of state, and their moral character. If it is true that there are no moral laws "by nature"; if legality is not a natural condition but an artificial one; then what does this entail for those actors, those statesmen, who are charged with establishing and maintaining these artificial, civil conditions? Can one establish a civil condition simply and purely by legal means? Is this not begging the question of where and how these laws emerge? But if the civil condition has uncivil conditions of possibility, then should statesmen not adopt a "reason of state" in their actions, a reason that excuses the use of execrable means in the pursuit of a higher good? Are statesmen, in times of necessity, allowed to bypass the rules that hold for most people? Since the publication of *The Prince*, the divorce of politics from morality has received the name of "Machiavellism." Undoubtedly, this part of his book has led to the fiercest debates. Here, again, the problem of application of rules comes to hand to explain what may have motivated Machiavelli to break so decisively with previous moral thinking. Machiavelli engages in an exercise of re-describing the conditions under which rules apply: if he excludes natural law, then he may have done this in order to let us see that our adherence to rules can be otherwise motivated, perhaps by our natural desire for freedom and creativity, which may require competition where previously collaboration was called for; which may require the protection of coercive measures where previously religious authority and persuasion were deemed to be sufficient.

In the last thematic section of *The Prince*, Machiavelli's concerns climb to the highest philosophical and theological-political levels: what is the cause of human happiness or unhappiness? Is there anything that we can finally do to secure our wellbeing in the world, or are we at the mercy of chance? Does divine providence exist and does it have a political meaning? These questions are discussed in Chapter 8 of the *Reader's Guide* in light of the same problem of rule-following that has guided us so far: if the validity of rules is context-dependent, then what is responsible for sudden changes in the relevant contexts? Is it chance, or God, or something else? Does human evolution, or adaptability to changing circumstances, exclude or require political revolutions?

The *Reader's Guide* concludes in Chapter 9 with a discussion of the reception and influence of Machiavelli's *Prince* in modern political thought. The very different ways in which *The Prince* has been received in the last 500 years is often a function of which of its structuring problems is highlighted. Machiavelli has been understood as a "teacher of evil" because he relativized moral considerations in politics. But he has also been understood as a great defender of the liberty of people because of his argument that the state ought always to have as its basis a free people in arms. Because of its emphasis on the productive character of social and class conflict, *The Prince* has had a fundamental impact on the way in which the socialist and communist movements understand the hegemony of the bourgeoisie and the chances for revolution. Lastly, the overriding concern in *The Prince* with the security of the state was decisive in the doctrine of "reason of state" that was extremely influential for the modern understanding of the art of government until the emergence of liberalism.

CHAPTER THREE

The seduction of a prince

The Dedication to Lorenzo de' Medici

Is *The Prince* a treatise of political science, dispassionate and scientific, value-neutral as we would say today; or is it a "tract for the times," a piece of propaganda, a work of political passion? Or is it an elaborate exercise in rhetoric, intended to educate both princes and citizens about the true civic virtues? We can begin tentatively to answer these questions by reading the "Dedication," since in this text Machiavelli says for whom and to what purpose he wrote his book.

During Machiavelli's life there were no publishing houses, and universities did not remunerate their professors for writing books. The usual way to get something out of a book was to dedicate it to a patron, of which Machiavelli had, during his time in exile, none that he could count on. Instead, he dedicates his book to two different Medici scions: in a letter he wrote to a friend announcing that he was working on *The Prince* he mentions his intention to present the work to Giuliano de' Medici, who was rumored to receive a principality. Later, he changed his mind and dedicated it to his nephew, Lorenzo de' Medici, who was the ruler of Florence. Both Medici were not officially princes but were thought by Machiavelli to be on the way to becoming so. This "Dedication" inaugurates the riddle that *The Prince* became for all subsequent readers: what could it mean that this model republican citizen was also the infamous "author" of *The Prince*?[22] If the book was written in a republican spirit, is this masterpiece of modern political science or wisdom nothing but an elaborate exercise in irony and perhaps satire, a bitter joke played on the rich and powerful? Conversely, if Machiavelli seriously meant to help the new princes of his world gain and sustain their power, then does it turn one of the masterpieces of modern political science into a monument of opportunism, hypocrisy, and moral relativism? Or did Machiavelli have in mind another political project entirely, a project for which the creation of a new prince was the means but not the end?

Princes tend to be busy people not known for dedicating much of their precious time to underlings and their insignificant gifts. Thus the "Dedication" is comparable to the ten-second pitch that an unknown scriptwriter, if lucky, gets to present to the famous producer. The first thing Machiavelli says is that his little book contains all the "understanding of the deeds of great men" (Dedication, p.40) he has gathered from his experience and studies, which cost him much trouble. He underscores that he is giving the prince "knowledge and understanding," later even saying that the book demands to be "diligently studied and read." Machiavelli is thus offering an education to the young prince, a lesson to a student. That doesn't sound like such a great gift; who wants to sit in class all day when one is at the top of the world already? But Machiavelli sweetens the bitter pill in two ways: first of all, the study time will be brief. Just like this *Reader's Guide* is meant quickly to give you the knowledge to achieve good marks, so Machiavelli says his little book will "give you the ability in a very short time to understand all that I ... have known and understood." No need to waste time in dusty and moldy libraries, like humanists and academics, to get what you want.

But Machiavelli does not explain what is so great about the gift of knowledge. Why does he think this gift is better than riches? A frequently used word in the "Dedication" is "greatness." Machiavelli wants to make sure that "you should arrive at that greatness that fortune and your other qualities promise you," and he offers a sure way to reach such greatness by giving "rules for the conduct of princes." That sounds doubly presumptuous: not only is Machiavelli styling himself as a teacher of the prince, but he is going to give him rules. He is addressing his book, or script, to a Medici, and the Medici pride themselves with having run the great city of Florence for more than a century from behind the scenes, hence their accumulated knowledge about power, ruses, conspiracies, etc. would be hard to match, especially by a young and humiliated second-rank secretary of the defeated Republic.

A Medici may have accepted this kind of talk only from a court philosopher with a certified claim to the superior, nearly divine, wisdom of Plato and Aristotle, both of whom advised princes. But for a Medici this was a wisdom to be enjoyed while on holiday from the hard work of governing others, a wisdom that makes no claim to know better than the prince how to rule, but only serves to appease the ruler's conscience. Had Machiavelli presented himself as a philosopher, like Ficino, he might at least have been received with some sympathy; after all, court philosophers are useful for keeping up appearances. Additionally, the mixture of modern experience with knowledge of the ancients was one that a Medici would have already known from the chancellors and humanists they selected to guide Florence; and a Medici would also have been familiar with the format of Machiavelli's book, a guide for princes, a book in the well-known "mirror of princes" genre. Nothing so far would have struck him as novel, nothing would have whetted his appetite to read on.

It is at this point that Machiavelli explains away, with a single brilliant image, the prince's misgivings. This is the heart of the pitch. Machiavelli refers to the technique of Renaissance artists: "just as those who sketch landscapes place themselves low in the plain to consider the nature of mountains and of high places, and to consider the nature of low places they place themselves high atop the mountains, similarly to understand well the nature of peoples it is necessary to be a prince, and to understand well the nature of princes it is necessary to be of the people" (Dedication, p.40). The entire point of the book is encapsulated in this one image that refers to how pictures are made, to painting techniques. Since to this day the Medici owe their immortal fame to the patronage of great artists, Machiavelli's self-presentation as an artist or technician of politics is not a bad gambit. And just as a painter must take into account how her work will be perceived, so Machiavelli suggests that to attain greatness in politics one must know the effects of one's actions on the subjects who are affected by them. What matters is managing the consequences of such power on the common people, not the moral intention behind the deeds (intentions are always good, outcomes vary). Greatness requires that the prince enter into an alliance or agreement with the common people.

This model of power based on alliances was central to Lucretius' view of the world; he calls them *foedera* and describes all of the universe as a gigantic enterprise of building alliances between atoms.[23] But the Medici, who started as merchants and bankers before they became princes and Popes, would also have understood Machiavelli's image in economic terms: just as in any market arrangement between buyer and seller, the optimal result is achieved when the seller knows what the buyer knows and conversely. That way, both are sure to get what they seek from their arrangement. As we shall see later, Machiavelli proposes that the exchange medium between a prince and a people should not be money but security. Already implicit here is the first lesson: the power of the prince rests with the people's opinion of the prince. Thus Machiavelli introduces the democratic bias of modern politics generally.[24]

The knowledge that makes the alliance between prince and people possible is achieved by moving between two perspectives, the perspective of the prince and the perspective of the people. It requires a theorist able to scale the heights and descend to the lows of both the prince and the common folk. Machiavelli's book therefore opens the communication between those in power and those without power, making this communication the very secret of greatness in statecraft. The most important painting technique invented and perfected by Florentine Renaissance painters was linear perspective. This technique permits the exact measuring of distances between things at a distance by bringing them onto the same geometrical plane. Linear perspective, in this sense, destroys the aura of natural things and cultic objects, the sensation of an immeasurable distance no matter how close one approaches them. Machiavelli's science destroys the aura of power, the sense that the source of power is immeasurably distant from the common folk. Authority is based on this illusion of unbridgeable distance; so is religion. Machiavelli's knowledge is such that it destroys once and for all the mystery of state, the aura of authority. Power is no longer shrouded by mystery, by miracle, by wisdom with which priests and kings shrouded it and made it inaccessible to everyone else. The world of politics has been disenchanted; it has lost its magic. Machiavelli brings new rational rules to compute power as surely as the rules of bookkeeping compute profits. *The Prince* brings the power mechanism up close, breaks it up, and rebuilds it according to a first sketch of the analytic-synthetic method Hobbes would later deploy systematically.

But the destruction of distance also has a comic side: when the sacred is brought up close and revealed as profane it becomes an object of laughter, if not of derision. Tragedy is about not seeing what one ought to see; comedy is about seeing what one ought not to see. In this sense, *The Prince* is a book that mixes scientific earnestness with ironical intention, and for that reason Rousseau's and Spinoza's quip that Machiavelli wrote a book on princes intended for revolutionaries remains true.

STUDY QUESTIONS

1 Do people in power need objective knowledge about political reality or is this knowledge a threat to their hold on power?
2 Philosophers tend to have no power, and yet there is an old tradition according to which philosophers should advise those in power, and Machiavelli belongs to this tradition. Why is the right way to address those in power such a crucial issue if one seeks to be an advisor of powerful people?

CHAPTER FOUR

Acquiring state

Chapters 1–6

The "Dedication" promises greatness to anyone willing and able to read and apply the teachings of the book. The title of the first chapter specifies what is required to achieve greatness: the acquisition of the state. But what does "state" (Italian: *stato*) mean for Machiavelli? Is it the same thing as what we today mean by the state? The first sentence of the book tells us that "All states, all dominions that have had and do have command over men, have been and are either republics or principalities" (chapter 1, p.41). This definition of the state is by no means innocuous. Terms like "state," "republic," and "principality" would have been familiar to Machiavelli's contemporaries, but the definition itself already contains a revolutionary claim that his contemporaries could not have expected.

One can think about this opening gambit in two ways. As a modern scientific treatise, Machiavelli's definition of the state must be proven through its construction of the concept of "state." Just as in modern geometry, the true definition of a figure is that which permits the construction of that figure, such that the truth of its definition lies in the construction itself. Machiavelli's definition of the state is thus verified in the construction of the concept of state over the following chapters of the book (until Chapter 15). The book intends to "fabricate" the state before the eyes of the prince, enabling him or her to imitate this construction in reality. What is true is only what can be effectively made.

At the same time, *The Prince* is also a work of rhetoric. Machiavelli must demonstrate that he knows the art of persuasion at least as well as those humanists who wrote advice books for princes before him. He is a latecomer in the genre. Since the argument he is about to proffer is one he knows will shock his audience, Machiavelli must also be careful to make his case, and not just claim that a "state" can be made from nothing by following his new rules of statecraft. In this sense, the opening sentence of *The Prince* is an exercise in rhetoric establishing Machiavelli's argumentative organization of his material or subject matter in such a way as to construct the best argument possible for the skeptical eyes of a judging audience.[25] So, let's examine more carefully this crucial first line of the book.

Machiavelli's first readers would have understood the Italian word *stato* to mean what we in English still refer to as "status," a person's social standing in the eyes of others. Having status is the cause of respect, admiration, and also envy in others. The more status one acquires, the greater one is. Status is something possessed by persons. More concretely, it is the hold that one person has over other persons and things. A professor, for instance, is endowed with a certain status before his or her students. The status "professor" disposes students to pay attention to him or her, even before they have stepped into the classroom. This same status leads them to presuppose his or her grasp of the material, and they know he or she has a certain power over them as persons because they are compelled to come to class, behave in a certain ritualized fashion there, and to sit for tests and exams in which they shall be judged by him or her. This status can be quickly lost, of course, if professors have no idea what they are talking about or if students find them boring, if they abuse their position in any way, if they are unfair judges of the student work, and so on.

Machiavelli's contemporaries would have also understood "state" to refer to something which in English is still retained in the expression "the state of the nation." The expression refers to the condition of a country: is it in good or bad health? State here refers to the sum of policies and institutions that maintain or ruin the welfare of the country. A "statesman" is anyone who is charged with keeping the community in good condition. Hence the many references Machiavelli makes to the art of medicine, especially in chapter 3 of *The Prince*; a statesman is like a doctor for the community; he or she is called on in times of crisis to decide on the best treatment for the health of the political body, whether an operation is needed, what needs to be cut out when; and politics is as bloody as medicine. "As the doctors to a consumptive say, during the beginning of his illness it is easy to cure and difficult to recognize, but, with the passage of time, if no one recognizes or medicates it at the beginning, it becomes easy to recognize and difficult to cure. So it happens in matters of state" (chapter 3, p.47).

These meanings of the word *stato* are no longer sufficient to capture what we mean by the state today. For us, the state is not the possession of a single individual or group of individuals but an abstract juridical "personality," an impersonal organization that represents the interests of us "all" and makes out of our many little communities or families one all-embracing society. Nowadays, most of us are upset when we realize that the state might become the property of a single person or group or political party. We institute regular and competitive elections for important government offices, set up an independent judiciary, and create an autonomous civil society characterized by a competitive free market in order to assure the state belongs to no one person or group of persons, but represents society as a whole.

So Machiavelli's first thesis is that all states are either the possession of one, in which case it is called a principality, or of many, when it is called a republic. To have "state" means to have "command" over the population of a certain territory. In principalities, this population is composed of subjects. In republics, it is composed of citizens. There are only two types of command over a population: the monopoly of command, which we refer to as a principality; or command shared among many, which we refer to as a republic. In the contemporary parlance of political science, what Machiavelli refers to as a republic is called a "polyarchy."

What is revolutionary about this way of thinking about political institutions? Machiavelli claims that greatness comes from knowing how to command other human beings, to have empire (*imperio*) over them. During the medieval era, the great political battles were fought between the Church and the Empire, between the holders of "authority" (unarmed priests) and the holders of "empire" (armed kings). Strikingly, from our modern perspective, no emperor ever managed to best the Church's authority. Ultimately, obedience was not due to weapons or force, but to a non-violent compulsion based on religious faith. The final reason for this situation is that medieval society had no centralized organization of command, no "state" (in Machiavelli's sense of the term). Society itself did not depend on the machinery of a centralized, bureaucratic state, but was instead composed of interlocking and hierarchical networks of laws which regulated the actions of different orders or "estates" of people: common law for commoners; civil law for citizens; canon law for members of the Church; natural law for all living beings; divine law for all divine beings; eternal law for God alone. Medieval society was not a state-based society; it was a society of law.

When relations between people are regulated by law, the most important values are peace and justice: the avoidance of violence and correct adjudication of legal disputes. Religious authority should take care of the former; courts of justice should take care of the latter. The threat of punishment for transgressing laws has a place, but it is ancillary to the different jurisdictions. There is no space for a "state" that, by virtue of its monopoly on the use of violence in the name of the community's "freedom" and "property," issues unified, valid legislation, and thus lies effectively beyond the reach of both religious authority and common or natural law.[26] This idea of the state is, partially, an invention of Machiavelli. Although we now take it entirely for granted, it was in *The Prince* that this new idea of power, based neither on authority nor on law, but on command backed by a legitimized use of violence, saw the light of day. As we shall see, popular support of the state is Machiavelli's solution to the problem of legitimating violence without appealing either to authority or to law. But this point belongs to a discussion of how to maintain state, rather than to acquire it.

When Machiavelli asserts that all states are either principalities or republics he is unceremoniously discarding two other venerable ways of thinking about political organization. The first of these was invented by classical political philosophy. Plato, Aristotle, and Cicero all thought that a political relationship between people was not a question of command but a matter of "constitution" (*politeia, res publica*). They believed that every member of a community was best suited for a specific function, and political organization concerned distributing and coordinating across the community in the name of the general or common good of all members. This ordering and distribution was the work of a "constitution." For classical thinkers, all political life was by definition "constitutional." If the community happened to be run by individuals who disregarded the constitutional division of power, who did not care for the common good, then it ceased to be a true community, a form of communal or political life, and became a "tyranny." Tyranny disordered communities by assigning merits and functions at the whim of the tyrant, and not in view of what was best for the community as a whole.

Today we tend to have the opposite intuition: the less power is centralized in the hands of a legitimate state, the more people are allowed to take advantage of others and the more anarchic society appears to us. Perhaps we tolerate this "tyrannical" behavior of the state because, unlike the ancients, we have stopped believing that the role of political constitution is assigning ways of life. Instead, we let everyone figure this out on their own and demand that the constitution merely protect our free choices as long as they don't harm the freedom of choice of others. The state can protect this liberty only if it is sufficiently centralized and strong. Machiavelli was concerned with how to make such a state in the first place.

For Plato, Aristotle, and Cicero the big question was how to assign the important functions of the community; who was in charge of the "regime," of steering the community. A regime could be composed of one person, a few people, or many. If the regime distributed offices and made laws in accordance with the "constitution," then the regime was a good one. It received the name of monarchy, or aristocracy, or republic, depending on the number and social standing of the persons filling its offices. If the regime ran the community by transgressing its "constitution," then the regime was bad; monarchy degenerates into despotism, aristocracy degenerates into oligarchy (the rule of the rich), republic degenerates into "democracy" (by which was meant mob rule).

In letters written around the time he was composing *The Prince*, Machiavelli says that he wants to put into the booklet everything he knows about the craft of state-building [*arte dello stato*] (Letters, April 9, 1513 and December 10, 1513; O 2, p.240 and p.296). We now see that he meant to set rules not for what ancient political philosophers called "constitutional" or political life, but for what they called "tyranny." Plato, Aristotle, and Cicero thought tyranny was by definition incompatible with stable institutions and fixed rules of conduct. For them, political science could only mean the science of constitutions, not the science of tyranny. The audacity of *The Prince* is that it prescribes rules for the previously uncharted territory of a field understood to be outside reason. That is why Machiavelli often insists on the novelty of his enterprise (although he took care to learn many useful things from the criticisms and descriptions that ancient writers, mostly Aristotle, leveled at tyrants).

But Machiavelli says something even more radical in the first sentence of the book: if republics, and not just principalities, are also forms of "state," then what the ancient philosophers called "politics" or "constitution" or "republic" does not entirely correspond to any social order found in reality. In reality, politics has always been about establishing "states"; real politics has always had a tyrannical dimension. Both principalities and republics, autocracies and polyarchies, are variants of what ancients called tyranny; yet they are successful or stable variants of tyranny. Holding on to the difference between a tyrant and a monarch, between a democracy and a republic, is illusory and must be given up entirely if we are going to understand how states and statesmen really work. Machiavelli doesn't quite say this directly, as no one would have understood him had he done so. All previous political treatises, without exception, always taught that statesmen must behave like kings and avoid being tyrants, assuming a real difference existed between these two. Machiavelli moves in the other direction. States always start tyrannically and the problem is how they legitimate themselves. Only Machiavelli's followers, Hobbes and Spinoza, had the boldness, a century later, to explicitly announce the news by naming this legitimate tyrant the "sovereign"; and there are two possible sovereignties: either of the people or of kings, either republics or principalities.

Apart from classical political philosophy, the monotheistic or Abrahamic tradition provided a second venerable way of thinking about politics, starting with the Pharaoh Akhenaton in Egypt, then Moses and the Israelites, then Jesus Christ, and finally the Prophet Mohammed. For this tradition, all communities are organized around a central point of coordination that cares for the common good, much like a shepherd takes care of his flock. The political system of sacred kingship develops from this concept. As a religious conception of monarchy, it is distinguished from the classical sense of constitution by the fact that it is a personal kind of rule rather than a political-legal form of rule. In sacred kingship, one shepherd, one person, is charged with the salvation of the herd because this person is supposed to know best what each single member of the herd needs in order to attain their salvation. No system of law can make this subtle distinction between individuals and administer to each the care or sacraments they require to be safe forever.

The crucial feature of this kind of rule is that, like a shepherd, the monarch must be an entirely different kind of being than his flock; he must have some super-human attribute; he must be in contact with some form of absolute wisdom or transcendent truth, which we shall call simply "God". In the Western tradition two basic political institutions developed from this model of religious monarchy: either the king is also a prophet (or follows what the prophets tell him), or the king relates to God through a special institution representing the Kingdom of God on earth, and this is the Church. In Judaism and Islam, the preferred solution tended toward the prophet-king; in Christianity it took the form of a Church–king combination. Western medieval political thought is such a complicated affair for us to understand, not only because it is a form of society without a state, but also because, at a certain moment starting in the twelfth century, the political ideologies that were drawn up to legitimate either kings or Popes or city-states became a hopeless jumble of both models of rule, the philosophical-constitutional and the religious-monarchical one.

Machiavelli wanted to wipe the slate clean with respect to this tradition too. That is why, in the first sentence of his book, he takes care to say that no monarchy can be a "state": states are either principalities or republics. This is crucial. It is important not to identify a monarchy with a principality.[27] Monarchies, in the proper sense of the term, always derive their claim to power from a divinity, from the "charisma" or gift of rule a god bequeaths to his chosen "son." By their nature, monarchies claim to be "eternal" because eternity is the source of their power, namely, God.[28]

For Machiavelli, principalities have no claim to eternity and instead rest upon the ability of the prince to acquire and maintain command over a population. Such a modern prince may call him or herself a "king" or a "queen" but this honorific name changes nothing about the reality of their power and of its sources. For

Machiavelli, the source of this power is the people, who either obey or disobey the command of the prince, who either fear or despise the prince. And popular opinion, as the ancients knew all too well, is a fickle thing; it is as far removed from eternal wisdom as can be. That is why neither the Greek and Roman political philosophers, nor the defenders of divine kingship, could ever conceivably favor a democratic form of power. Today, on the contrary, we think that the only legitimate and stable kind of state is the one that rests on the opinion of the people. In part we owe this incredible revolution to *The Prince* and its exclusion, on principle, of divine monarchy as a form of "state."

But is Machiavelli simply brushing aside, as sheer nonsense, the combined wisdom of Athens and Jerusalem in the first sentence of his book? In a sense that is just what he does, because basing power on the common people as opposed to on the wise few is a gesture as revolutionary as Copernicus' discovery that the earth moves around the sun and not the other way around. But in another sense the first sentence of Machiavelli's book simply states a hypothesis asking for verification. He has to convince his audience that divine monarchies or philosophical constitutions never existed, and for that reason he appeals to history, in terms of both his lived experience and what ancient historians have to say about state building. History is thus a double process for verifying his hypotheses. This task fills the first seven chapters of the book, the first unit of the book.

Machiavelli begins with monarchies. Monarchies are merely hereditary principalities; and these are shown to be absolutely vulnerable to violent overtaking. There is no eternity with monarchs. If a monarch wants to keep what he or she acquires, his or her "state," then he or she must obey the rules of statecraft. This is the topic of chapter 3. But what about republics: why are republics also a form of state and not a "constitution"? To prove this point, which in effect requires him to pit his wits against the considerable opinions of a Plato or an Aristotle or a Cicero (no minor endeavor), would take him too far afield. Machiavelli acquits himself of this task by dedicating a longer book to the topic, namely, the *Discourses on Livy*.[29] It is obviously different for the many to have command over the many, as happens in a republic, than for one to have command over the many, as happens in a principality. At the same time, it is incorrect to think that between a principality, as

Machiavelli now understands the term, and a republic there exists an abyss. For Machiavelli, both remain species of one and the same thing, namely, of a state. It is a mistake to think that principalities refer to a state of "unfreedom" and republics to a "free" civil condition; these are myths propagated by ancient republicanism that Machiavelli is equally eager to dispel, as I shall show below. Although Machiavelli cannot go into details about republics now, he feels obligated to address the problem of how ancient philosophers understood constitution, which he does in chapter 6.

As we see, then, chapter 1 sets out the structure of the entire first half of the book: since command is not given by God but is acquired by a prince, clearly the first thing to understand is how princes acquire new states. We start from the case of a hereditary prince who already has a state and is intent on expanding his holdings, acquiring a new territory and thus forming a "mixed principality" (chapter 3). The population in the new territory is either accustomed to being commanded by another prince or not (if the state happens to be a republic); this is the topic of chapter 4. Then Machiavelli discusses the case of someone acquiring a state without first being prince of another state; this can be achieved either with one's own arms and by one's virtue (chapter 6) or by another's arms and by fortune (chapter 7). The discussion of acquiring states through fortune opens up another unit of the book.

Teaching kings a useful lesson

The third chapter of *The Prince* is very long, as Machiavelli has a lot to prove. He not only wishes to show his reader why starting from monarchies is no way to think about acquiring a state; he is also interested in settling a personal account with a particular monarch, namely, the French king Louis XII, who invaded Italy during Machiavelli's lifetime and whose ministers humiliated him when he came asking for military aid during his first diplomatic mission to France. The Medici princes to whom he dedicated the book were brought up in the conviction that their power depends on the favor of a powerful monarch; they also know Machiavelli's republic fell because of monarchs; Machiavelli must show the

Medici that his knowledge is more powerful than the French monarch. A lot is at stake in this third chapter. Machiavelli must capture the princes' attention.

The topic is "mixed principalities," that is, territories that are additions to one's principality, and are either other principalities or other republics. Machiavelli first distinguishes between types of territories: either they speak the same language or have similar customs as the prince's state, or they are foreign. In the first case all that is required to acquire and maintain the territory is that "the bloodline of the former prince be eliminated" (ch.3, p.44) while maintaining the old orders and not raising taxes, in this way assimilating the new territory to the old principality. In the case of foreign territory, the prince can only maintain it either by living there himself, for this brings the new prince closer to the occupied people, or by colonizing—but never by occupying it militarily, for in this way "he is much more offensive, because he harms the whole state by moving his army and its lodgings about ... so that each person becomes his enemy" (chapter 3, p.45). Third, the new prince should follow a politics of alliances with the weaker powers in the territories in order to weaken the stronger powers. Machiavelli goes on to explain how the Romans successfully occupied and destroyed so many of the surrounding monarchies in establishing their Republic: "For the Romans did in these circumstances what all wise princes should do" (chapter 3, p.47). Since, as he claims, both republics and principalities are forms of states, it is no problem to model one's state on a successful republic and apply these rules to a principality, as Machiavelli does here. We will see throughout the book that the distinction between republics and principalities blurs: the nature of politics is the same whether in principalities or republics, and thus Machiavelli's modern political science can discover its rules by studying both.

Next, Machiavelli examines the actions of the French king in Italy to test the rules he has discovered. Machiavelli's treatise offers rational rules, a technique or craft, to acquire states. If rulers are foolish enough to invade other countries without following these rules, they perish. Machiavelli illustrates his point by using the example of the failed invasion of Italy by the French king. Louis XII's decisive mistake was that, rather than aiding the weaker powers that sought alliances with him (like Florence), he helped the strong powers in Italy, especially the Church in the guise of

Cesare Borgia, and also the Spanish, who he invited into Italy in order to partition the kingdom of Naples. Everything here is in the rhetoric: Machiavelli first presents the rules, then he shows how the king obeyed none of them and lost his state: "Thus King Louis lost Lombardy because he did not observe any of those rules that have been observed by others who have taken provinces and have wanted to keep them" (chapter 3, p.50). And Machiavelli ends on a personal note: "For when the Cardinal of Rouen told me that the Italians did not understand war, I replied to him that the French did not understand states, since, if they understood them they would not allow the Church to come into such greatness." He seems to have taken particular relish in saying this to a Cardinal.

So power depends on knowledge of certain rules. These rules form a certain practical knowledge, and Machiavelli, following ancient usage, calls this knowledge "prudence." But whereas prudence for Plato or Aristotle or Cicero promised the achievement of a "happy life," a "good life" in the approving eyes of other citizens, other "good men," who lived under a constitutional regime, Machiavelli refers here to the prudence of a tyrant, intending to guide him or her in winning the state and succeeding in a world populated by unscrupulous, violent, and rapacious nobles and despots, aggressive city-states intent on keeping other cities in their territory under their rule, and above all by perfectly oiled war machines driven by foreign kings devoted to expanding their domains.

Machiavelli knows that rules by themselves do not magically produce greatness, just as the technique of perspective drawing does not by itself make a Michelangelo. Great art is not the result of a mechanical application of rules. Rules do not apply themselves. Two other factors come into play: rules must always be applied in particular, contingent situations, full of opportunities and dangers one cannot foresee (something Machiavelli calls *fortuna*), which one cannot master. Since rules do not apply themselves, when and which rule to apply is a matter of one's own capacity or virtuosity to interpret the situation and decide what is required by the situation (a capacity that Machiavelli calls *virtù*). The art of state is defined in this chapter by virtuosity or artistic energy in the employment of violence. All artistry is violent: it requires the destruction of old forms, of old traditions, as much as the creation of new forms, of new ideals. The art of state, the art of creating new states where old states stood, requires violence, and *virtù* is therefore the artistic, rule-bound employment of violence and force for the sake of achieving command over a group of people living in a given territory.

If order were not an artistic creation (of nature as much as of human beings), if order were the result of a "natural law," as the teleological vision of the universe advocated by both the ancient and the Christian philosophers suggests, then establishing a state would come naturally to men, it would not require violence and force (or better: establishing a state would be something only wise men can do—see Chapter 6). Keeping a state, likewise, would require a good ruler merely to follow natural law which guarantees that goodness ultimately rules in this world. Machiavelli does not believe in such a world; for him there is no natural law, and this means that rules are applied in an exceptional state, not in a normal one.[30] Normality, stability, regularity: all this needs to be conquered; it is not natural. There is no guarantee one can succeed. Later we shall see that Machiavelli believes a prince must learn not to be good but to use violence as the animal uses it: in an artistic, measured use of aggressiveness.

Above all, the fragility of hereditary principalities (the form of state that comes closest to being "natural"), which are often swept into oblivion by violence, proves there is no natural basis for the social order. That something is "old" or "inherited" does not make it well-founded. Plato and Aristotle would have agreed. But they would have said that it is possible to give a "rational" foundation to political order that is also "stable," and this "rational" foundation is "natural" law: the belief that what is right and what is wrong is somehow contained in the nature of things themselves. Every nature of every thing, no matter how small or how big, is normative because some things are good for it, others are bad. But what if such "nature" does not exist? What if everything that exists is a contingent assembly of particles, which in some relations continue to exist and in other relations cease to exist, and that all of this is ultimately determined by their adaptability to unpredictable situations? On this picture of nature, which corresponds to the modern scientific worldview, neither the ancestral nor the "natural" offers a foundation for a stable order. Only violence, craft, genius, and luck make order possible. Kings, beware! Do not trust custom, do not trust wisdom; these cannot prevent your ruin in this world of atomic swerves. The only road forward is innovation, the art of creative destruction. And Machiavelli is the new kind of guide for this new road to worldly success.

Chapters 4 and 5 indicate the real aim of Machiavelli's attack and the real distinction between the principality he is proposing and the idea of monarchy: namely, a territory with a central government in the person of a prince, or a feudal monarchy in which the king is but the highest nobleman. From the perspective of the state, the latter is much more difficult to deal with because each nobleman is a potential prince; even if one eliminates the bloodline of the prince, other nobles emerge as potential princes. This is why the Roman Republic never quelled rebellions in Spain or France until "the memory of those principalities was eliminated through the power and duration of empire" (chapter 4, p.53). This insight leads Machiavelli to chapter 5, where he distinguishes between the occupation of a republic and that of a principality. In the latter case, elimination of a bloodline will be sufficient because the people "do not know how to live in freedom" and can become subjects again, but in the case of republics, a people will never willingly choose subjection because "there is greater life, greater hatred, more desire for revenge. Nor does the memory of their ancient liberty ever allow them to rest, nor can it, so that the most secure way is to eliminate them or live there" (chapter 5, p.54). Princes had better stay away from republics, or, if this is not possible, they had better learn to attain power by becoming "civil" princes within a republic. This is ultimately what the Medici needed to relearn, and this is the goal Machiavelli is leading them toward in *The Prince*, culminating in chapter 9 dedicated to "civil principality."

Founding fathers and other myths

Since Plato, the role of the true statesman is to found a community based on the rule of law or on a constitution. For the ancient Greeks, as well as for modern Americans and Europeans, some legal constitutions—especially those which set up a state that lasts for a long time and reaches considerable power—seem endowed with near superhuman political wisdom or prudence. The individuals who designed these constitutions, one thinks, must have been political geniuses, demigods or at least near to the gods. Today we still call these people "Founding Fathers." Not only Plato, but also Aristotle and Cicero—that is, the greatest representatives of ancient political philosophy—thought that a republic had its origin in a man of superior wisdom and also eloquence, who persuaded by his rhetoric the uncultivated and dispersed human beings to congregate within city walls and obey common laws, giving to each what is theirs, and thus establishing a civil condition.[31]

In order to claim that republics are also types of states, and like other states also require violence for their foundation, Machiavelli needs to address this traditional vision of foundations. He does so in chapter 6. Unlike the discussion of monarchies, which presuppose the possibility of transmitting power by biological descent, and thus considers only new principalities as additions to old ones, here Machiavelli delves into the theme of "principalities that are wholly new, both in their prince and in their state." This is the ideal type of innovation in politics because the person becomes prince in and through the creation of a new state; in this sense, the prince himself constitutes the state, and the state that he creates, conversely, constitutes his or her status as prince.

Machiavelli says that "this event—becoming a prince from being a private man—presupposes either virtue or fortune" (chapter 6, p.55). In this chapter he examines the first case, a prince that founds a new state on the basis of virtue alone. Later he will examine the opposite possibility, of a prince who attains power through good luck or fortune. He proceeds to list these founders of new states: Moses, Cyrus, Romulus, and Theseus. They are the mythical founders of the Hebrew Republic, the Persian Empire, the Roman Republic, and Athens, respectively. To a Medici and a Florentine, the appeal of Rome and Athens as model cities would have been self-evident. Moses would also have been important given that Savonarola wanted to establish the model of the Hebrew Republic in Florence, and statues of Biblical heroes and heroines adorned the city. Cyrus was something different; he appealed directly to a Medici because of the Platonic connection: Xenophon, a contemporary of Plato and follower of Socrates, wrote the *Education of Cyrus* and made this emperor an ideal leader.

What all of these founders share is that they are all law givers: "if their actions and life are examined, it is not seen that they got anything from fortune other than opportunity, which gave them the material so as to be able to introduce into it whatever form they chose" (ch.6, p.55). Here is the pure case of innovation, where virtue is maximal and fortune is minimal, in so far as fortune here merely amounts to access to a pure matter, previously uninstructed and unformed, awaiting the founder's introduction of whatever orders he or she wishes. Essential to Machiavelli is, in the last instance, what it means to introduce such form, what is required to establish a state.

The task of founding an entirely new state is an enormous one, and for that reason these figures are considered semi-divine, that is, on an entirely different plane than mere mortals. Fearing the Medici ruler might be turned off by these seemingly unattainable examples, Machiavelli reassures him: there is no choice for human beings but to "walk in paths beaten by others and they proceed by means of imitation" (chapter 6, p.55). For that reason "a prudent man should always enter by paths beaten by great men and imitate those who have been the most excellent." The goal for the reader of *The Prince* is not to establish something as great as the Roman Republic or the Persian Empire; the task at hand is something more modest (what the task is, Machiavelli has not yet ventured to say—this only happens in the last chapter of the book), but none the less requiring the reader to "aim high," over and beyond the stated aim, like the "prudent archers" who "place their aim much higher than the intended place, not in order to reach a place so high with their arrow, but to be able, with the help of so high an aim, to achieve their goal" (chapter 6, p.55). Today as well, it is customary in great republics to encourage young school children to "become president," not because we really want them to do so or believe they can, but because one can achieve something in life only if one has set one's aims high enough.

But there remains a second objection: all these founders were superhuman heroes, so how could a Florentine prince possibly rise to their level? Here for the first time Machiavelli broaches the fundamental question of the relation between religion and politics. Of the mythical founding fathers, Moses is unique because he founded not only a new state but also a new religion. Additionally, Moses is guided directly by God: "he was a mere executor of the things that were ordered of him by God" (chapter 6, p.55). If Moses is the ideal statesman, then must not the prince also be a prophet? And how can one decide to be a prophet? Is this not

God's decision and gift? Does this not mean that politics is a matter of divine providence?

Here Machiavelli makes another shocking claim. First of all, Moses "should be admired, if only for that grace that made him worthy of speaking with God." It is not entirely clear what Machiavelli is hinting at here, but one possible meaning is gathered from reading the Hebrew Bible: there one finds that, at first, all the Hebrew people heard the voice of God at the foot of Mt. Sinai. But since the voice was too terrible for them, they were incapable of dealing with this responsibility and selected Moses to go up the mountain and speak to God and receive His orders. Thus Moses became prince thanks to the "grace" awarded him by the people. In a sense Machiavelli is here simply translating the Roman adage, *vox populi, vox dei* (the voice of the people is the voice of god) back into the Bible. For the true statesman, the voice of God is the voice of the people.

Furthermore, Machiavelli adds that when one considers the actions and lives of the other founders, and of Cyrus in particular, "they will appear no different from those of Moses, who had so great a teacher" (chapter 6, p.55). This sentence has often been read as if Machiavelli were being ironic, as if Moses simply invented his conversation with God. But it can also be read as an indication of Machiavelli's appreciation for the project of a Platonic theology. Machiavelli is saying that God's political science, as exemplified in the work of Moses, and Platonic political science, as exemplified in the work of Cyrus, are not so different. Machiavelli is simply referring to an old belief of "ancient theology," according to which Plato was a student of Moses. As far as Moses is concerned, for Machiavelli, God's wisdom is an exalted political science, nothing less, nothing more. The Christian idea that theology and politics belong to two different spheres and establish two different institutions at odds with each other, the Church and the state, is a false teaching. All religion is civil religion, that is, all true religion is religion that motivates subjects of states to be good citizens.[32]

Founders acquire a state by introducing "new orders and methods"; in other words, constitutions. They constitute their own people, and when they succeed their state is well-founded because they produced the foundations themselves. That is why Machiavelli claims founders need only be given the opportunity of finding a dispersed group of people to unite by giving them a political identity and a political future: "It was therefore necessary for Moses to find the people of Israel in Egypt, enslaved and oppressed by the Egyptians. ... Theseus would not have been able to demonstrate his virtue had he not found the Athenians dispersed" (chapter 6, p.56). Founders "establish their state and their security" by literally making for themselves a people. This is an endeavor requiring entire peoples to adopt a new way of life, a new religion, a new education.

The difficulty here consists in inculcating in a people these new ways of life, of which they have no previous experience. "One should consider how there is nothing more difficult to treat, nor more doubtful to succeed in, nor more dangerous to manage than to make oneself a leader who introduces new orders. For the introducer has as enemies all those who are doing well under the old orders, and, as his defenders, all those who would do well under the new orders are lukewarm. This lukewarmness arises in part out of fear of their adversaries, who have the laws on their side, and in part from the incredulity of men, who do not truly believe in new things unless they see that they arise from solid experience" (ch.6, p.56). A new religion means a new aim in life, a new purpose, a new set of commandments. Founders who give new constitutions are necessarily illegitimate, their actions are necessarily extra-constitutional. They break with previous legal and religious orders so as to institute new ones, but the act of institution falls outside both old and new legal orders; it falls in a state of exception. We are back to the same theme that Machiavelli inaugurated in chapter 3, namely, that the application of a rule does not stand under another rule. This is the paradox of all constitutional regimes, and therefore it shows, once again, that all politics begin from an illegitimate condition that must be rendered legitimate. The ancient, "constitutional" understanding of politics reveals itself, in the end, to be part of the *arte dello stato*.

The condition of beginning a new constitutional order by breaking with a past order or religion requires founders to be "prophets": they bring a new religion and at the same time they delineate a future for their people.[33] Machiavelli witnessed this dynamic in action during his lifetime, when he saw the rise of the prophet Savonarola in Florence. But his awareness that a constitution requires a religious appeal to grab hold of a people and mold them does not itself rely on a religious narrative, on a transcendent

God who acts as guarantee of the success of the new religion. The prophet may "see" a future for its people, but history is something else entirely. History is characterized by chance, which escapes foreseeability and providence, as he argues in Chapter 25.

That is why the use of religion in politics does not escape the general rule of state acquisition, namely, "whether to carry out their work they need to pray, or whether instead they can use force" (chapter 6, p.56). The distinction is between "armed prophets" who succeed and "unarmed" ones who fail. Machiavelli applies the distinction to the case of Savonarola: "he was ruined in his new orders when the multitude began not to believe him" because he could not order them "in such a way that when they no longer believe, one can make them believe by force. Moses, Cyrus, Theseus, and Romulus would not have been able to make their peoples observe their constitutions for long if they had been unarmed" (chapter 6, p.57). Religion in politics does not obviate the knowledgeable use of violence but renders it necessary: no founder of a civil religion ever succeeded on the force of persuasion alone. Jesus Christ is no exception: his disavowal of violence required him to say that His kingdom is not of this world, and his followers had to give to Caesar what is Caesar's, because, as Machiavelli says in the *Discourses on Livy*, they were too weak to punish offences against them.

The chapter dedicated to the founders of republics, therefore, shows the necessity of "tyrannical" beginnings for republics as well as principalities, and closes on the same note. Machiavelli writes not of a mythical founder but of a real tyrant, "Hiero the Syracusan," who "has some similarity" with the previous founders in that he did what they did, namely, provided new foundations to his power: when "the Syracusans were oppressed they elected him as their captain, hence he was worthy of being made their prince" (chapter 6, p.57). It is not by chance that Machiavelli chooses Hiero. He is referring to Hiero II, an ally of Rome in the wars against Carthage; but it is hard to avoid the suspicion that he may be also referring to Hiero I, who lived some two centuries before, and is the subject of Xenophon's dialogue of the same title, in which at issue is how a tyrant can attain happiness if he is everywhere threatened. What characterizes Hiero II, according to Machiavelli, is that once in power, thanks to the favor of the people, he sets out to make his state self-sufficient by making "alliances and soldiers that were his own" so that "on such a foundation" he could "build any building whatsoever" (chapter 6, p.57). Machiavelli does two things here. First, he brings down the figure of the innovator to a realistic, historical possibility—in effect, the very situation of the Medici dedicatee, who is also rising to the position of prince thanks to the support of citizens. Second, Machiavelli begins to delineate the possibility of what he will soon call a "civil principality," namely, a form of principality in which a private man is brought to power through the favor of an oppressed people. What he has not yet done is explain how such a civil prince maintains the state he acquires through the good fortune of the popular election. This is the topic of the next three chapters, which open up a new section of the book.

STUDY QUESTIONS

1 Is Machiavelli right to claim that a republic is a species of state? Or did classical political philosophy have a point when it distinguished republics from states?

2 What kind of rules does Machiavelli's political science discover? How do these rules differ from moral precepts? In what kind of a world do these rules apply?

3 Why does Machiavelli believe that ancient constitutions were based on violence? Why is this fact important when it comes to thinking about why modern constitutions are products of revolutions?

CHAPTER FIVE

Securing society

Chapters 7–10

Founding fathers must depend on their own virtue because they are not confronted by an already existing people, they do not face a pre-existing society. There is simply no one "there" to elect them, to lift them into office, to support them while in power, to topple them when they become dissatisfied. In the beginning, everything depends on the charisma of the leader because there is no routinization of power, no institutional framework within which power can be transferred according to certain mechanisms, and so on. Before these mechanisms can exist, at the moment of foundation an undisputed leader, an armed prophet who has the capacity to carry "his" people along no matter how difficult the path ahead seems, is necessary. At the mythical beginning of states, the human material is inert; it is mere clay in the hands of the founders and legislators. Institutional mechanisms of power-sharing come about only because this initial situation cannot persist. Charisma is not inheritable or transferable in any way. If a lasting state is to emerge, then its charismatic origin must make way for a rational-legal structure of power. Wise founders know this, and for this reason they bequeath to their followers not a successor but a constitution, a legal mechanism to guide a people in their selection of the most adequate leaders in the indefinite future.

Machiavelli knows that behind the founders' wisdom and virtue lies necessity. The truth is that the "savages" that the mythical political heroes organize into a "people" are anything but inert matter; on the contrary, they are alive and rebellious. A people constantly throws up challenges to those in power, either because it resists their commands or because it wants to compete for their position and status. Unless these challenges are met by the constitutional structure of the state, the state will not last. No one prior to Machiavelli had identified this autonomy of society with respect to the state. No previous political thinker had so clearly seen the sociological and economical presuppositions of politics that we take for granted today. Classical political theory, especially Aristotle, was aware of the dangers posed by widespread inequality of possession in a society, but only in terms of the assumption that society is a collaborative effort which seeks to harmonize the different functions people are "born" to fulfill. As Plato says in the *Republic*, a city is made possible thanks to justice, and justice means allocating to each their "own" function, the one they are meant to fulfill by "nature." The true statesman is the one who understands how to recognize and distribute functions according to the most harmonious mix. Machiavelli no longer believes in this function-based conception of society. For him, every individual is born the son of chance and must make him or herself into whomever they want, given enough luck and virtue. Society should be constructed in such a fashion as to best use the diversity of luck and virtue within the people, rather than attempting to stifle it.

The new section of the argument, composed by the Chapters 7 through 9, introduces the absolute novelty of a pre-political, socio-economic condition of a divided and antagonistic people that all statesmen or princes confront once they attain power. This "fact" of pluralism and conflict changes everything because, from here onward, the power of fortune or contingency in politics occupies center stage. Thus, even as Chapter 7 seems to continue the earlier discussion concerning the acquisition of state, in reality Machiavelli is already speaking of the maintenance or security of the state. Indeed, when a prince comes into power through good fortune—as in the case of Cesare Borgia, discussed in Chapter 7— there is hardly a question of acquisition: the only real question is how this new prince is to secure the state he or she has acquired. Here, for the first time Machiavelli, reveals the most important presupposition of his new political science, namely, the claim that matter is never inert but always alive and characterized by desire. Given the right conditions, matter can shatter any form that is imposed on it and generate a new form for itself. Machiavelli's approach to politics is materialist because matter (the people) always trumps form (the prince's state). One could even put it more radically: there is no definitive political form or state that can contain this matter of a people. The desires of the people are threatening to whoever wants to impose a political form on them. Therefore the prince's primary task once he acquires state becomes securing his or her position in this state.

The vocabulary employed by Machiavelli in Chapters 7 through 10 is centered on the idea of security as opposed to the idea of virtue. If the accent in the first six chapters is placed on the need for aggressiveness, suddenly, in Chapter 7, the prince is placed on the defensive. The *security* of state, the *economy* of violence, these are what is essential in the *arte dello stato*. But now we are speaking of the possessions of two political actors, not just one. For the prince, the possession that must be secured is the state. Yet Machiavelli inscribes this security within the larger context of securing the possessions of the subjects of the state, those who alone provide the prince with a stable foundation, if he is to have any foundation at all. As he writes: "I shall conclude only that for a prince it is necessary to have his people as a friend, otherwise, in adversities, he has no remedy. ... And let there be no one who strikes back at this opinion of mine with that trite proverb that 'He who builds on the people builds on mud'. For that is true when a private citizen builds a foundation on the people and allows himself to think that the people will free him if he is oppressed by his enemies or by the authorities. In this case, he could find himself often deceived, as happened at Rome to the Gracchi. ... But if he is a prince who builds on the people, who is able to command, and if he is a man of heart, who does not take fright in adversities, and does not fail in his other preparations, and who with his spirit and his orders keeps the populace inspired, he will never find himself deceived by the people, and he will judge that he has built good foundations" (chapter 9, pp.70–1). Contrary to all previous Western political thought, Machiavelli argues in Chapters 7 through 9 that the prince can institute his state, and consolidate his position or status, only on the foundation provided by the support of the people, rather than on the noble elements of society, the "great" or "wealthy," the élites. Curiously, though, it is also here, alongside this highly democratic claim, that he argues the true statesman must be a "good" tyrant.

The *arte dello stato* places contingency at the center of politics, and political prudence becomes entirely a function of security. We are familiar with this belief today because we think it is the duty of the state to protect our rights and property. Indeed, today the legitimacy of the state is in many ways a function of the security it provides us, but in Machiavelli's time the centrality of security as the primary goal of politics was a complete novelty. Previous political thinkers wanted to hold on to the illusion that power depends on translating what is necessary and true—whether divine providence, the course of the stars, or the truth of the moral virtues—into reality, and not on dealing with contingency. Security becomes central to politics only when Machiavelli discovers that disorder, disagreement, and conflict are productive principles for society, so long as they are properly channeled: "For in every city these two different humors are found, whence it arises that the people desire not to be commanded nor oppressed by the great, and the great desire both to command and to oppress the people. From these two different appetites there arises in the city one of three effects: principality, or liberty, or license" (chapter 9, p.69). Here we have an origin of states that is entirely distinct from the mythical one of the "founding fathers": all states have their origin in social conflict. Or, as Marx put it a few centuries later, all history is the product of class conflict.

The importance of Machiavelli's revaluation of social conflict for the development of political thought in modernity cannot be overemphasized. All modern social sciences, if they are to be scientific, must begin by taking into account the fact of social division, whether this is interpreted in terms of class conflict, or in terms of the "fact of pluralism," or simply in terms of the rational pursuit of self-interest. The point is that, for modern political science, social division is primary with respect to political unity.[34] Machiavelli is the first political theorist to claim that civil association (and thus politics) exists on the ground of passionate and conflictual relations, and not on the ground of reasonable relations of cooperation: antagonism and competition, not consensus and collaboration, are the essence of the social bond.

The second major innovation lies in the character Machiavelli ascribes to social antagonism. For if the antagonism were simply one between agents interested in ruling over one another, it would be possible to show (or, at least, since Socrates out did

Thrasymachus in the first chapter of the *Republic*, think it possible) that such antagonism cannot produce a social bond, but only its opposite: the degeneration of society. But Machiavelli's concept of social antagonism is immune to this objection. For him, people and nobles do not designate natural kinds; instead, whoever speaks and acts out of a desire to dominate assumes the standpoint of the nobility, and whoever speaks and acts out of a desire for non-domination assumes the standpoint of the people. One and the same individual may therefore occupy these different standpoints at different moments. A minority can act as a people, just as a majority can be ennobled. (In the *Discourses on Livy* Machiavelli dedicates much space to the analysis of both of these possibilities in the history of the Roman Republic and in the passage to the Roman Empire.) Furthermore, what counts as desiring non-domination is not predetermined, nor does it have to be univocal. People and nobles are entirely differential terms and not static identities. The primary social conflict is therefore irreducible to the contest over who should rule. The conflict that traverses society is not a struggle over who is going to rule; it is a conflict between those who want to rule and those who want no-rule. "Without doubt, if one considers the end of the nobles and of the ignobles," argues Machiavelli, "one will see great desire to dominate in the former, and in the latter only desire not to be dominated" (D, I, 5). Machiavelli conceptualizes the possibility of political unity, and thus the possibility of political rule, from the perspective of a necessary social division on the matter of rule, that is, a necessary conflict over the question not of who should rule, but of whether and how there should be rule at all. In so far as this question remains open, the social bond is maintained as a conflictual bond.

From Machiavelli's viewpoint, every modern state attempts to answer a demand raised by the continual conflict between domination and non-domination with what can only ever be a partial and contingent response. That is why, from this viewpoint, it cannot be left up to the state to determine when, where and on what terms its rule is to be politically contested. Machiavelli puts forward a general principle of modern politics, according to which any political order, if it is to be constituted and legitimated, must also be open to its deconstitution and delegitimation. The only legitimate political order is the one that can be made to suffer its own radical contingency. Politics is only the interpreter or translator of social difference and conflict. Since it is possible to translate form into freedom or freedom into form, two sorts of instituting strategies characterize modern political life: either what Machiavelli calls, in the above quote, "principality," or what he calls "liberty" and is embodied by a "republic." *The Prince*, with its theory of the civil principality, and the *Discourses on Livy*, with its theory of the modern republic, give two complementary illustrations of this general principle of modern politics.

When read closely and comparing the texts, Chapters 7, 8, and 9 treat exactly the same process of securing the prince by way of securing the people. On its face, Chapter 7 concerns the acquisition of state through fortune and is exemplified by Cesare Borgia; Chapter 8 concerns the acquisition of state through "wicked deeds" and is exemplified by Agathocles, the tyrant of Syracuse; and, finally, Chapter 9 concerns the acquisition of state through the election of its own prince by the people, which Machiavelli baptizes a "civil principality." But in reality all three chapters are moments of one and the same discussion, namely, how to secure for the acquired state the foundations, in the people, that will permit it to last as long as possible. How to institute a state that lasts in time: this is the new normative horizon of modern political science.

Once this fundamental contingency of political rule becomes the horizon of political action, two kinds of politics emerge, both of which are necessary, and neither is sufficient in itself. The first kind of politics seeks to minimize the insecurity of rule by founding a state that lasts through time. Machiavelli's theory of the state as a "civil principality," sketched in Chapter 9, gives a figure to this politics. The durable state is only possible if the prince takes the side of the people against the nobles, and the people, in turn, become the ground of the state and support its rule. That the modern prince or state is, from the start, preoccupied with providing "security" (to itself and its subjects) follows directly from the radical contingency of its ground. Machiavelli argues that "security" can be achieved only by securing, but not suspending, the prince's rule or command over the population of a determinate territory. The civil prince is the name for a state that founds itself by making the practice of rule a matter of mutual security between the governing and the governed.

Machiavelli explains this logic of security in Chapter 8, when he praises the tyrant Agathocles for knowing how to make "good use" of cruelty. Agathocles mastered the economy of violence needed to secure the people, and through the security of the people build steady foundations for his state.

"Cruelties may be called 'well used,' if it is permissible to speak well of evil, when they are done all at once, *out of the necessity of securing oneself* [*la necessità dello assicurarsi*]. ... In seizing a state its occupier must run through all those offenses that it is necessary for him to commit, and commit all of them at once, so as not to have to renew them every day, and to be able, *by not renewing them, to secure the men* [*assicurare gli uomini*] and to win them to himself by benefiting them. Whoever does otherwise ... need always keep his sword in hand. Nor can he ever *rely on his subjects* [*fondarsi sopra li sua sudditi*] since they, because of their fresh and continuing injuries, *can never be sure of him* [*assicurare di lui*]" (chapter 8, p.68, emphasis mine). The Italian term repeated three times by Machiavelli, "*assicurare*," shows without a doubt his insistence on the new prince's fundamental need to achieve security for both the state and its subjects. This generalized security follows three stages. In a first stage, the new prince secures him or herself against potential rivals, just as exemplified by Cesare Borgia. This stage institutes what Max Weber calls the "monopoly of violence" characteristic of the modern state. In a second stage, the new prince must secure the people against the extra- and infra-legal desire for domination by the powerful in society, that is, the nobles. Historically, this stage refers to the destruction, on the part of the modern state, of feudal relations of domination (but not the elimination of the noble desire to dominate, which is re-channeled). In the language of republican politics, we speak of this stage as the state providing security from the *dominium* (personal domination) of the "powerful" in society: élites, wealthy individuals or corporations, racist majorities or misogynous husbands.

The third and decisive stage transforms the tyrant into a civil prince. In this stage the prince must assure his or her subjects with respect to his or her status (*li sua sudditi ... assicurare di lui*), so that they will continue to support the prince's state whenever the prince's possession of it is threatened. Translated, again, into the language of republican politics, this task corresponds to providing security from the *imperium* (legal or impersonal domination) of the state itself. Only by achieving this last task does the prince or state, properly speaking, become a "civil" principality or a civil society, as the prince will have brought "civility" to the relation between individuals and groups in society. Though the term "civil society" was only coined a few centuries later by the Scottish philosopher Adam Ferguson, its basic characteristics are prefigured in Machiavelli's discussion of a tyrant who fulfills the requirements of republican politics by bringing security to a people.

Cesare Borgia, as depicted in Chapter 7, carried out these three steps in achieving the security of state. Inverting the procedure that he used to chastise the French king Louis XII, where Machiavelli first describes the rules then verifies them through the case of the king, here he first illustrates the way Cesare Borgia proceeded and only later, in Chapters 8 and 9, draws out the abstract rules by a process of inference. Cesare Borgia is the experiment that Machiavelli stages in order to verify his theory of the "civil prince," itself a term Machiavelli was the first to use.[35] If, in the first part of the book, Machiavelli discovers new political rules for states-manship, but lacks anyone to apply them, now in this second section of the book he provides an exemplar of the application of these rules of the new political science, yet without a theorist to make them explicit. Through the construction of the figure "Cesare Borgia" and the explanation of his actions in terms of a new concept like "civil principality," Machiavelli also presents himself as a necessary addition to the political genius. But what is the new role of a theorist like Machiavelli?

The third stage of security in reality stands for the discovery of ideology as crucial to modern politics. The new role of the theorist, inaugurated by Machiavelli, is both to provide and to unmask ideologies. Perhaps the most important achievement of *The Prince* up to this point is demonstrating that civil society requires systematic deception on the part of the prince's state. The exercise of a monopoly of violence, even if wielded on behalf of the people against those who engage in domination, cannot but project a "bad," domineering image of the state that fails to reassure its subjects. Therefore, Machiavelli argues that the modern state or civil prince must follow the path of simulation and dissimulation (see Chapter 18) in order to construct for itself an appearance of "goodness" that stands a chance of satisfying its subjects. To do so, the modern state has to become what Louis Althusser calls an "ideological apparatus."

The "ideological" component of the modern state refers to its capacity to legitimate the violence it exerts in the name of securing legal rights for its subjects. The modern language of rights, in fact, cannot be separated from the state-centered politics designed to achieve the security of rule. In this sense, when Marx asserts that "security is the supreme social concept of civil society … the concept that the whole of society is there only to guarantee each of its members the conservation of his person, his rights and his property,"[36] he is simply voicing the fundamental intuition grounding the modern idea of rights, from Hobbes through Kant and Mill. Machiavelli's new prince becomes the "civil prince" only when he or she begins to secure the rights of his or her subjects, because only in this way can the prince secure the state, both for him or herself and for the state's subjects.

In *The Prince* Machiavelli offers a memorable illustration of the sense in which the state's monopoly of violence, exercised in the first two stages, dissembles itself in the form of rights, the establishment of which institutes a "civil society." Cesare Borgia used the ruthless Remirro del Orco in order to violently repress the nobles in the region. As such he achieved the second stage of security, but left the people questioning the goodness of the prince, and whether they might be next on his hit list. In order to reassure them, Cesare Borgia had to "drop" the sword from his hand by cutting off the arm that held it: "Then the duke [Cesare Borgia] judged that such excessive authority was not necessary, because he worried that it would become hateful. He appointed there a civil tribunal, in the middle of the province, with a most excellent presiding judge, in which each city had its own advocate. … [And] to purge the spirits of those people and to win them wholly to himself, he wanted to show that if any cruelty had taken place, it was not caused by himself, but by the harsh nature of his minister. And seizing an opportunity for this, in Cesena one morning he had Remirro placed in two pieces in the town-square, with a piece of wood and a bloody knife at his side. The ferocity of that spectacle left those people at once satisfied and stupefied" (chapter 8, pp.61–2).

Cesare Borgia's "spectacle" is intended to communicate that the goal of mutual security between the people and the state shall take the form of right.[37] This is why Machiavelli emphasizes the institution of a civil and supreme court of justice, with all the trappings of modern political representation, as the climactic moment in founding a civil society. In civil society, mutual security is not one right among many but is the content of all rights; it is the meaning of right as such. For instance, in *On Utilitarianism* John Stuart Mill defines a "right" as something composed of two elements: injury or harm, and a consequent punishment. To have a right to anything means that society, through the state, must back this right with the threat of violence (or harm) for whoever harms society by violating its persons (i.e., the socially recognized identity of citizens). Modern right is what it is by virtue of its need to (publicly) coerce those who (privately) coerce, to violently punish those who use violence without the authorization of the state. This violence of right is what Mill names the "force of law." Here, this internal or necessary relation between the recognition of rights and the punishment of those who do violence, is exemplified by Borgia's own violation of De Orco's violent kingly arm, the latter representing the *imperium* of the office-holder that the civil prince must secure on behalf of its subjects and in the name of the state. De Orco's severed body, displayed in a public space next to a bloody sword, symbolizes the sense in which violence will be removed from the civil body politic in the state of right.

Although the civil prince manages to transmute violence into right, the trace of pre-rightful violence, anterior to the institution of the modern system of right, cannot be entirely erased from the system. The persistence of this trace remains apparent in two related features of the modern state of right. First, even if the modern state of right requires the destruction of the feudal nobility it cannot and should not eradicate the "noble" desire to dominate, since without it the people would no longer require the state's protection. Rather, the system of rights re-channels the desire to dominate into the "private sphere," as a desire for possessions, and everyone is now allowed and encouraged to pursue this desire within the limits of law. Second, the state always retains the capacity to exert pre-rightful violence. At the end of Chapter 9, Machiavelli hints at this, arguing that civil principalities, in times of emergencies, need to "ascend from a civil to an absolute order," despite the difficulty this may pose for a prince who wishes to remain faithful to the legal system he has instituted. Machiavelli here is indicating the problem of what will shortly thereafter be called the "coup d'État," or what nowadays we call the "state of exception." Hobbes was the first to make clear that the state (or Leviathan) can only protect the rights of its subjects if it itself is not party to a contract with them; for it is the state's capacity to use violence against those who break the social contract that makes this contract possible. Only the state, according to Hobbes, gets to keep its natural right to use a pre-rightful violence to guarantee the social contract and ward off the state of nature.

Machiavelli is very clear that a "civil principality"—that is, a state whose mission is to "civilize" society and social relations—cannot be achieved unless the prince allies him or herself with the people as opposed to the nobility. The state is "civil" if it follows the desires of the people against the desires of the great. What is important here is the concept of "honesty" as the guarantor of intent: "Beyond this, one cannot in *honesty* satisfy the great without injury to others, but one may so satisfy the people, for the end of the people is more *honest* than that of the great, since the latter want to oppress and the former want not to be oppressed. Moreover, a prince can never secure himself against a hostile people since they are too many, but against the great he may secure himself, since they are few" (chapter 9, p.70). Thus the civil prince may be a tyrant, but he must be an "honest" one because he defends the "honest" interests of the people and not the "rapacious" interests of the great. Honesty is the bourgeois virtue: it is the fundamental virtue of free commerce and free thinking. Honesty is the virtue that "polishes" society and turns it into a "civil" society.

And yet, in order to give honesty a chance, the new prince must act in ways that are not "honest": "one cannot call it virtue to kill one's fellow citizens, to betray one's friends, to be without faith, without compassion, without religion. These modes may be used to acquire rule but not glory" (chapter 8, p.66). So Machiavelli speaks about Agathocles, whom he calls a "most excellent captain" though "his bestial cruelty and inhumanity … do not allow that he should be celebrated among the most excellent men" (chapter 9, p.66). But why not? The answer lies in the fact that the civil principality, although founded on a people, is still not a republic. The civil prince must cast his or her lot with the people if he or she is to win their support, but this does not mean that the people are princes, as happens in a republic. The civil prince is securing his or her command, but this is not the same as producing a political system that truly satisfies the people's desire not to be ruled or dominated: the civil principality is not yet a state of non-domination, a republic.

So why do people accept the civil prince? How is the civil prince capable of deceiving them and why do they let themselves be deceived? In his book on republics Machiavelli makes it clear that a civil principality cannot entirely satisfy the people's desire for freedom. His claim is that the modern prince is, by definition, the political actor who interprets and addresses the demand not to be dominated or oppressed as a call for security under a system of impersonal law. Freedom from domination becomes freedom from interference: the generation of formal equality under law is the central strategy through which the prince appeals to the people, providing them with a simulacrum of their desire for no-rule. This simulacrum is nothing but civil liberty, the securing of which establishes the new prince as the civil prince. Machiavelli's theory of the civil prince makes possible modern liberalism, understood as the creation and sustenance of the social and political systems of negative liberty through which the modern state secures for itself a foundation in the people.[38] In Renaissance Europe, and particularly in Florence, Machiavelli witnessed the early emergence of the free labor market, the positive rational-legal order, and the recognition of individual rights: what was missing was a conception of the state capable of producing, through a logic of security, such a civil society out of the feudal system of power. Machiavelli's *Prince*, and in particular his conception of the civil principality, is the first such proto-liberal theory of the state. But Machiavelli was also conscious of the fact that, by accomplishing its goal of legitimating domination, liberal politics must inevitably corrupt the people's desire for freedom as an end (political freedom), only providing freedom as a means (civil liberty). Unless modern political life is capable of periodically returning to a republican mode, the final result of such corruption, or of bourgeois honesty, is what Machiavelli calls "license," and what today we would perhaps call libertarianism or neo-liberalism.

Chapter 10 concludes this section by providing a transitional moment from the discussion of security to the discussion of war. The new or civil prince, as Machiavelli understands it, is the prince who founds his power on the people by making the people rely upon him for their security. War is, then, the test of how well a prince has secured his foundations: "whether a prince has a state sufficient that he may stand by himself if he needs to, or if instead he always needs to be defended by others. ... I judge that the ones who can stand by themselves are those who are able, whether through abundance of men or of money, to put together a proper army and to fight a battle in the field with whomever comes to attack them" (chapter 10, p.72). Machiavelli then informs his reader that the next chapters (Chapters 11–14) will specify what it means to depend on one's own army.

STUDY QUESTIONS

1 Is conflict or cooperation the basic fact about society? What are the consequences in each case for the function of government?
2 Should law serve to bring about security, or should law make people into better persons? Or does law have other functions as well?
3 What is Machiavelli's idea of "civility" (as in: civil society) and what are its conditions?

CHAPTER SIX

Arming the people

Chapters 11–14

Machiavelli closes his discussion of acquiring and maintaining a state with a puzzle: how is it that the Catholic Church, an "ecclesiastical principality," survived every imaginable challenge and yet seems to be a state that follows none of Machiavelli's newly discovered rules of political science? The clergy "alone have states and do not defend them. They have subjects and do not govern them" (chapter 11, p.73). Priests are usually the opposite of soldiers, thus a state composed of priests cannot have at its foundation the conduct of warfare. But that is exactly what Machiavelli is about to argue: unless a state makes warfare its central business, it shall perish. So it is imperative that he resolve the exception posed by ecclesiastical principalities before tackling the topic of the proper relation between politics and war.

How could the Catholic Church, a state that knows nothing about war, survive and prosper amongst war-mongering kings, republics, and empires? This question resembles the familiar question often posed in relation to the Jewish people: how could they survive, and indeed outlast other peoples, despite being continuously persecuted? Is this evidence that special divine providence exists; that God has a "chosen" people? Is it true that God somehow loves more those people who "surrender" themselves to Him, and therefore He protects them in mysterious and supernatural ways? Machiavelli considers this possibility: "since they [ecclesiastical principalities] are ruled by superior causes that the human mind is unable to reach, I shall leave out speaking about them, for since they are exalted and maintained by God, it would be the office of a presumptuous and rash man to discuss them" (chapter 11, p.74). Machiavelli knows that he is being disingenuous here. He is all too aware that if such divine providence really exists, it undermines everything he will argue with regard to how a state must protect itself, leaving himself open to the objection, made by priests every-where and since time immemorial, that when confronted it is best to rely on faith. Jesus taught that it is better to offer the other cheek, and Socrates taught that it is better to suffer a wrong than to commit one because God or nature or karma will balance the scales of justice, though perhaps only in the next life. And in any case, it is always better to govern a "state" through prayer than violence. Machiavelli obviously does not believe this is the case. The section of *The Prince* that we are about to read is intended to refute such arguments (and in so doing drive home the point that it is always better to exclude priests from running governments).

But the question is more complicated than it seems, and Machiavelli is unwilling to rule out divine providence as a factor in history. Perhaps he has no knock-down arguments against the possibility of special divine providence: after all, when things really take a bad turn in our lives, the majority of us—even the most secular among us—nearly instinctively appeal to a higher power for guidance and assistance, perhaps, who knows, even whispering a prayer or two. Or, maybe Machiavelli thinks there is another way to make sense of divine providence, a way that aligns God's will with the proper development of your own forces, your own armies, even more than in praying to Him, as is discussed in Chapter 26.

Chapter 11 seems to pose the following alternative: either God is on your side and you do not need armies, as with the Catholic Church, or you are not sure whether God is on your side, and therefore must arm yourself well. If you are a prince, but lack a church, then you had better build yourself a good army. (Somewhat later, after the success of the Reformation, the modern doctrine of state sovereignty will also require the prince to get himself a church: *cuius regio, eius religio*, "whose rule, his religion.") Either God's favor or an army of one's own: there are no other forces on earth strong enough to withstand the ups and down of fortune.

But this is just Machiavelli's opening gambit. In reality, he does not believe in this disjunction between God and war. Maybe he knew Heraclitus' saying that "War is the Father of all things." Certainly, Machiavelli held to the Heraclitean belief that only becoming exists, that "you can never step in the same river twice." But for the moment he proceeds cautiously. First of all, as he explains in Chapter 11, even the Catholic Church, like every other principality, attained "greatness in temporal affairs" in the same way all new princes attain greatness, namely, by ridding the Papacy of those aristocratic families who set up fiefdoms within the Church by weakening the central authority of the Pope and opening his state to "factional" conflicts through cardinals. It helps Machiavelli's case, of course, that Pope Alexander VI was just such a prince, using his own son, Cesare Borgia, to better establish his hold over the territory governed by the Church.[39]

But Machiavelli wants to cast more doubt on the Christian belief that God and war are opposed. He had already begun doing so when in Chapter 6 he recalled that all great prophets have been armed prophets. Now, in Chapter 12, he continues this thought, claiming that mercenary armies "have no fear of God and no faith with men" (chapter 12, p.76), thus implying there is another more religious or pious kind of army. Here he also approvingly cites Savonarola's prophetic claim that, by allowing the French king to invade Italy, God was punishing the "sins of the princes." Though, Machiavelli adds, Savonarola did not know that the sins in question were the princes' unwillingness to raise proper armies (chapter 12, p.77). His general point is that military weakness is a "sin" punishable by divine justice.

Having more or less skirted around the obvious Christian objections to militarism, Machiavelli is now ready to fully transition from the section on securing the state to the section on warfare. He spells out the main thesis of this section of *The Prince* as such: "We have said above that it is necessary for a prince to have good foundations, otherwise of necessity he must be ruined. The principal foundations that all states must have, whether new or old or mixed, are good laws and good arms. And because good laws cannot exist where there are no good arms, and where there are good arms there should be good laws, I shall leave reasoning of laws and I shall speak of arms" (chapter 12, p.76).

A momentous revolution in political thinking is contained in this simple formula. In classical political philosophy, priority was always assigned to good laws or to the quality of the constitution of the state. The use of military force is only justified if the cause is the right one, and that means, if military force is used to defend the constitutional regime, the good laws given by the founding fathers. But why is the pursuit of war in the defense of a constitution a manifestation of "courage" while the organizing of an armed rebellion against such a constitutional regime is deemed "foolhardiness" or "recklessness"? Isn't military virtue a value in itself? This was a difficult question to tackle for classical political philosophy; both Alexander the Great and Julius Caesar seemed to pose tough counter-examples, just as Frederick II or Napoleon did for the Middle Ages and for the modern epoch, respectively. Aristotle, for example, felt compelled to distinguish between the prudent political leader (*phronimos*) and the crafty political leader (*deinos*), knowing full well it is often impossible to distinguish between them: were Lincoln or Churchill prudent or crafty when, in order to save their countries, they exceeded what their own constitutions permitted?

Machiavelli's approach to the age-old question of whether laws or arms are the most important foundation of a state is determined by his discovery of the nature of a people. For classical political philosophy, laws were deemed to be "good" not because they rested on the (majority of the) people's opinion, but because they came down to an uneducated people from the heights of human and divine wisdom; these heights could only be attained by the very few, perhaps only by one. But Machiavelli has just shown in Chapters 7 through 9 that, for a new principality (and every state is "new" in this sense), such superhuman wisdom is of little importance because it takes no account of the "matter" or "basis" of the prince's power, the people, who, on the whole, are far from wise. Since the prince must build his or her state on the people, he or she cannot begin from "good laws" that the people are unable to understand, since they lack the enlightenment of the founders. The new prince must begin by something that an uneducated people can easily grasp, and this is "good arms."

At first sight, there seems to be a simple way to understand why "good arms" should have priority over "good laws." What good is a just constitution, a great culture, or a thriving economy, if one lacks the strength to defend these achievements against external aggression? It seems evident that the first foundation of political, cultural, and economic greatness is a strong military. But is this really so evident? Julius Caesar and Napoleon were military geniuses who rose to power for the sake of defending republican constitutions, but ended up destroying them and setting up empires that led their peoples to ruin. Or, looked at another way, maybe all cultural, economic, and political achievements depend on successfully expanding one's dominion over territory, in fashioning an "empire," even as this process of empire-building may very well lead to the corruption of good laws. In either case, a strong military is not easily synonymous with a "good military" that leads to "good laws."

So what does Machiavelli mean by "good arms"? And why do "good arms" necessarily lead to "good laws"? Chapters 12 and 13 are dedicated to proving the thesis that all arms are either mercenary, auxiliary, or "one's own" (chapter 12, p.76; chapter 13, p.81). The only good ones are arms of "one's own": "I conclude that unless it has its own arms, no principality is secure. Instead it is completely dependent on fortune, since it does not have the virtue reliably to defend itself in adversities" (chapter 13, p.84). What distinguishes between mercenary and auxiliary arms, on the one hand, and arms of "one's own," on the other, is money. Whereas one can "buy" the former, one cannot purchase the latter. So here we find Machiavelli proposing a very strong hypothesis on the basis of his proper experience with building up an effective army for the Florentine republic from the Tuscan peasantry, and the disastrous consequences for Florence of relying on foreign armies. Put directly, Machiavelli hypothesizes that men and not monies win wars; money alone does not make for good arms.

Up until Chapter 12 Machiavelli spoke about the need for an army in a generic sense, without taking a position on whether it is more important to have "an abundance of men or of money" (chapter 11, p.73). But in Chapters 12 and 13 he drops all ambiguity. If a prince must buy his armies, then by definition this army is not "his own" but belongs to the highest bidder. And when the grim reaper is clearly visible ahead, no amount of money will drive a mercenary or auxiliary army to fight to the bitter end.

Machiavelli's thought here reflects a significant moment in the history of warfare: the transition from a feudal to a modern conception of war. Feudal warfare is essentially the "private" affair of the wealthy and powerful nobility; their armies were composed of the vassals of the feudal lord who offered their services to the lord in exchange for protection. The king's army was the summation of all these private armies, and the king relied on the allegiance of other nobles in order to keep the army under "his" control. The moment the nobles withdrew their support of the king, the king began to tremble on his pedestal, as we know from Shakespeare's historical plays. No feudal prince, in this sense, met Machiavelli's requirement for an army of "its own." Modern warfare, by contrast, is strictly a "public" affair; it is warfare conducted between states, not between noble families, and in such wars peoples fight against each other. (Nowadays we may be moving into a postmodern form of warfare, where armies are once again "privatized.") Thus, Machiavelli's claim that the new or modern prince must have an "army of its own" means nothing less than that this prince needs to have a people that "belong" to him. Machiavelli wrote at a transitional moment between feudalism and modernity, when new princes were building new states and needed armies to conquer these territories, but lacked peoples to fight with them for their state. As a result princes tended to buy the armies they needed rather than create them, with the predictable result that their new states perished as soon as they came into existence.

Machiavelli boldly proposes that the only way a new prince can hope to gain an army of "his own" is by arming his or her own people, their subjects. And only by arming the people (and disarming the nobility) will the new prince win over the allegiance of the people, de facto making this army an army of "his own." The hard lesson that Machiavelli teaches the new prince in these chapters is that it is impossible to develop arms of one's own without the aid of the people, which requires that the prince keep the nobility under check. That is why he concludes that "one's own arms are those that are composed of your subjects, your citizens, or your dependents: all the others are either mercenary or auxiliary. And the way to order one's own arms is easy to find, if one goes over the orders of the four men [Cesare Borgia, Hiero II, David, and Charles VII, the French king who defeated the English thanks to Joan of Arc] named by me above" (chapter 13, pp.82–4).

What do all these historical characters have in common? All of them gained arms of their own by defending the freedom of their people, especially the freedom of the peasants oppressed by the feudal lords. Peasants fight for their lords because they do not have weapons to defend themselves; the price they pay for their security is subjection to the feudal lord. If you arm peasants, you destroy their feudal allegiance to the nobles and free the people to form a new allegiance to the new prince. Here is the real reason that "good" arms necessarily bring about "good" laws. Good arms means a popular army, a people in arms, who are no longer forced to ask for the protection of the nobles, of the élites. From this condition follow "good" laws because these are laws that protect the people's freedom against the abuses of the rich and powerful in a given society. Once again the same pattern is revealed: when we think Machiavelli is at his most "tyrannical" (in relation to the standards of classical political philosophy), in this case in his privileging of good armies over good laws, he is in fact closest to becoming a republican, and indeed producing a democratic political philosophy. It is no coincidence that he refers to David's fight against Goliath as an example of a new prince who chooses to fight with his own arms (the sling) rather than with the heavier gear offered him by king Saul, since David was a hero of the Florentine Republic. In the *Discourses on Livy* Machiavelli is even bolder. There (D, I, 26, pp. 61–2) he cites David as an example of a new prince who, in order to found his state, must be willing to risk a social revolution; taking away from the rich (the nobles) in order to give to the poor (the people).[40]

The section dedicated to warfare ends with Chapter 14, as Machiavelli begins to discuss the character of the new prince, his theme in the next section. In this chapter Machiavelli tells the new prince that he or she must think about warfare all the time or face contempt in the eyes of soldiers because no one who is armed (soldiers) freely obeys someone who is unarmed (prince). To bolster this lesson he refers to Xenophon and his book *The Education of Cyrus*. Through this text, Machiavelli makes the point that great generals of the past (here: Scipio, the Roman general who defeated Hannibal) became who they were not only through fighting, but by imitating exemplary warriors of the past (here: Cyrus, the Persian emperor). And what made these soldiers models, besides their military exploits, was the fact that they were represented as exemplary by philosophers: "And whoever reads the life of Cyrus written by Xenophon recognizes afterwards in the life of Scipio how much that imitation brought him glory, and how much, in his chastity, affability, humanity and liberality, Scipio conformed with those things that had been written by Xenophon about Cyrus" (chapter 14, p.86). The Medici scion is Scipio, who needs to read Machiavelli's representation of the life of Cesare Borgia and imitate it in order to become a great general and prince. Thus Machiavelli tells us that his little booklet on princes follows the genre of the "mirror of princes" introduced by Xenophon. But this is itself a "game of mirrors" because, in the very next chapter, Machiavelli destroys the genre, breaks the mirror of the prince, by presenting an entirely new set of princely virtues that have little to do with "humanity" or "liberality."

STUDY QUESTIONS

1 Does reliance on a people's army lead to more or less aggressive militarism on the part of the state?
2 What is primary for Machiavelli: internal politics or foreign affairs?

CHAPTER SEVEN

The new prince goes through the looking glass

Chapters 15–23

Chapter 15 of *The Prince* opens the second half of the book. In the first half Machiavelli showed us what kind of a thing a state is and what needs to be done in order to acquire and to maintain it. His main point thus far is that the new prince lacks the kind of virtue that makes an entire people depend on him; on the contrary, the new prince comes into power through the favor of others, thanks to fortune. The task of the new prince is rendering his or her state as independent of fortune as possible by building it on foundations that can resist changes of fortune. To do so, the prince must make himself indispensable to the people, whom he or she relies upon to support his or her state. The question Machiavelli now poses is: "what kind of a person should be charged with state, what are the qualities or virtues needed in the new prince?" Or put another way: "what kind of virtue is required to beat back changes in fortune, to turn what is contingent into what is necessary?"

The second half of the book is modeled on the more than a thousand-year-old tradition of texts directly advising princes, the so-called "mirror of princes." By choosing to discuss princely virtues only after discussing the nature of the state, however, Machiavelli reverses the traditional ways these treatises generally proceed. The "mirror of princes" assumes the personal qualities of the prince come first, and the state comes second: state is a gift bequeathed to the statesman because of his or her moral virtue. Plato was the first to argue that the "good man" is the true king, even if no one happens to recognize his "office." You did not need to have state in order to be a true king. But this belief quickly leads to the more unsettling proposition that the "good man" (a.k.a. the philosopher) may never need to hold "office" in order to rule effectively. Perhaps the most effective government always goes on behind the scenes, such that all government is shrouded in *arcana imperii* or "mysteries of state." Maybe these mysteries are the real lessons a true advisor to princes ought to teach his pupils. This is probably what Ficino, the Florentine disciple of Plato, believed was his role with respect to the "shadow" government of the Medici "dynasty," over what was nominally a free city.

Machiavelli hated the very idea of a "mystery of state." The *arte dello stato*, or statecraft, he was developing is the antithesis of mystery; his technique of government is clear and distinct, above all to those who are subject to it. If today's governments run on statistics (which is an offspring of the *arte dello stato*), if no politician dares say anything in public without having some policy wonk covering their back, we owe this to Machiavelli's concerted destruction of the "mystery of state." Like Alice, he wanted to go through the looking glass of princes. But this meant bypassing the advice that a prince ought to be a good man, in order to bring to light what the "moral" mirror image kept from public sight for so long, namely, the governmental practices shrouded in the "mystery of state."

The humanist books on the "mirror of princes" that Machiavelli directed his treatise on principalities against did not directly refer to Plato, who was little known and less studied until Ficino's translations became more widely circulated. Instead, the humanists employed the widely studied and copied Cicero and Seneca, perhaps the greatest Roman moralists. Although Cicero hated Julius Caesar's desire to become prince of Rome, and Seneca praised his Roman emperor as a god on earth, both of them upheld the belief that moral virtue alone kept the statesman from becoming a tyrant. Their writings on politics further polished Plato's mirror of princes, making it impossible, for centuries, to see through its image and pierce into the truth that it hid, namely, that there is no difference between a prince and a tyrant.

In Latin, the word for virtue is *virtus* and contains the root *vir*, man. For the Romans, virtue was a form of manliness, connoting both humanity and strength. Strength keeps one's animal passions under control, while humanity is the trait that allows one to see in the other another oneself, and to treat them accordingly. For Roman moralists, strength and humanity are most perfectly combined in the highest moral virtue: justice, giving to each what is theirs. Both Cicero and Seneca argue that power and glory follow from moral virtue. Cicero says it best: "once upon a time men of good character were established as kings in order that justice might be enjoyed. For when the needy masses were being oppressed by those who had greater wealth, they fled together to some one man who excelled in virtue. ... This, therefore, is manifest: the men who are usually chosen to rule are those who have a great reputation among the masses for justice."[41] Similarly, Seneca argues at length in *On Clemency* that whoever has absolute power must use it in such a way as to be loved by his subjects, and this can only be achieved by judging both his friends and his enemies through the lens of mercy provided by divine providence.[42] The emperor of the world strives to understand the absolute interconnectedness of everything and "communes" with all of it (as "natural law" teaches), thus feeling only compassion for all things: fear and anger vanish; he no longer needs the sword to conquer. Seneca's virtuous prince was quite uplifting reading for Christian princes.

The belief that moral virtue grants state has a powerful and appealing logic to it: would people, despite their weakness and lack of security, give power and authority to someone who is not good or virtuous or merciful? Don't sheep want a good shepherd? But what if people decide they are being fleeced by their keepers? What if they decide to take on the wolves themselves? Then they might not want to elect a leader who is all mercy. Machiavelli is not interested at all in keeping a people in a state of weakness and deprivation, in a state of neediness. On the contrary, he has just argued for several chapters that, if the prince wants to maintain his or her state, he or she must rest his or her power on the foundation afforded by a people in arms. From this democratic perspective, it is safe to say that the new prince of this new state is required to show virtues other than justice in order to keep the subjects from being exploited and used as cannon-fodder to feed the rapacious appetites of the privileged few.

This radical change of perspective explains why Machiavelli structures his discussion of princely virtues (Chapter 15 through Chapter 23) directly in opposition to both Cicero and Seneca (and indirectly in opposition to the Platonic tyrannical teaching).[43] This may seem puzzling at first sight, given his praise for all things ancient and in particular for all things Roman. Some interpreters argue that Machiavelli followed Roman historians and scorned Roman moralists because the former were realists while the latter were idealists. This is, of course, partially true. But the important fact is that the Roman historians, by virtue of their subject matter, had no choice but to describe the qualities (the "virtues") of the Roman leaders and soldiers as these manifested themselves in continuous warfare over centuries as part of a concerted project of world conquest. Cicero and Seneca, the moralists, could afford to limit their descriptions of these same leaders and soldiers to their peacetime roles as Roman citizens and heads of households, having removed their bloodstained armor and put on lily-white togas. The soldier who returns to Rome only to refuse to play along with the farce of citizenship is the stuff of Shakespearean tragedies, not of the moralizing tales of Cicero and Seneca.

But whether moralists or historians, Roman thinkers alike agreed that the qualities that allowed Romans to win wars against foreign enemies were very different from the qualities needed to maintain a community of friends in a state of concord; after all, no one ever won a war by just showing justice and mercy to their enemies. Cicero himself came up with the famous maxim, *inter arma enim silent leges* ("in times of war, the laws are silent"). Justice and mercy reassert themselves once the enemy is defeated and peace needs to be sealed. Indeed, the Romans were masters of the art of turning conquest into peace by welcoming defeated nations as equal citizens of the Roman Empire: *pax romana*, the Roman style of peacemaking.

Machiavelli calls into question this distinction between a city at war with foreigners (empire) and a city in concord with its own citizens (republic). He has already shown that the new prince needs to develop an army of his or her own, and think about warfare all the time, especially in times of peace. The fundamental reason for this is the fact that a new prince always comes to power in a society characterized by an on-going struggle between the nobles and the people, between the rich and the poor, the oppressors and the oppressed. The prince must choose who is friend and who is enemy internally, in order to face the state's external enemies and friends. Indeed, in the *Discourses on Livy* Machiavelli shows that, in practice, the Roman Republic never upheld the distinction between war abroad and peace at home, since the Roman "mission" to conquer and civilize the rest of the world was ultimately motivated by the need to manage the class struggles at home. Be that as it may, Machiavelli's point is that the virtues of the new prince will have to be those qualities that secure victory for his or her alliance with the people in this social struggle against the privileged strata of society.

By way of contrast, if we inquire into what Cicero means by justice and injustice, he is adamant that justice does not mean "an equalization of goods. What greater plague could there be than that? For political communities and citizenships were constituted especially so that men could hold on to what was theirs."[44] But how did we get to the situation that a few families own most of the land and the majority of citizens and foreigners are indigent, not to mention the existence of slavery? Today many people are loudly asking where is the justice in letting 1 percent of the world population keep 90 percent of its wealth? Cicero does not bother to pose the question. Machiavelli is obsessed by this question. Yet he was prudent enough to put his thoughts about this state of affairs in the words of a Florentine plebeian revolutionary (whom he then openly reprimands): "all those who come to great riches and great power have obtained them either by fraud or by force; and afterwards, to hide the ugliness of acquisition, they make it decent by applying the false title of earnings to things they have usurped by deceit or by violence" (HF, III, 13, p.123). The wealthy and privileged classes of society, the new prince has to struggle against to establish his or her state, are not "good men": they are wolves in sheep's clothing.

So, the qualities or virtues of the new prince are relative to the qualities or virtues of the state, which is characterized by having its foundation in an armed people. If politics is war, as Machiavelli argued in the previous section, then the activity of founding and securing a state is carried out, at least partially, in a state of exception from laws and justice. Machiavelli follows tradition by calling this a dimension of "necessity" and opposing it to reason. There are extreme situations in which necessity requires one do what is wrong in the eyes of reason. The person who is able to perceive these situations and act accordingly is endowed with "virtue" according to Machiavelli. Because what is required in this state of exception is not what is usually termed virtue, interpreters often refer to Machiavelli's redefinition of the term by its Italian name, *virtù*, thereby signaling its distance from the ordinary, moral sense of virtue.

The existing genre of "mirror of princes" was based on the assumption, shared by classical and medieval political philosophy, that "natural law" exists; thus, it is rational for everything alive to pursue what is good and avoid what is evil. For human beings, due to their social nature, what is good generally takes the form of obedience to given laws (divine laws as much as positive laws). Natural law teaches that, in every situation that demands a decisive course of action, there is always a right and a wrong decision, a morally right answer, conforming to higher law or moral principle, which justifies the action taken, making it the right thing to do. In the picture painted by natural law, there is no room between human prudence and divine providence for a state of necessity or exception, and this is why human freedom is defined by prudence understood as the capacity to do the right thing at the right time.

Machiavelli rejects "natural law" in the above sense. All "good" laws are born from a situation of social and political conflict which is itself not ruled by law; the state of emergency or necessity is not itself an "exception" to the normal state of human affairs ruled by "natural law"—it is the rule. Machiavelli believes that the struggle for the state, the struggle to impose a civil condition where individuals can and must live according to the rules of law, is not carried out through the rule of law but in its absence.

On the assumption of natural law, the prince is simply required to be good (or just) and appear so to others, in order to receive the support of his or her subjects. Since the ultimate source of all goodness is God, this means that a charitable, merciful, and chaste prince full of religion accrues to his or her person both power and authority. Ultimately, this way of thinking models the statesman after the priest and the magician. We saw in previous sections Machiavelli's consistent desire to separate statecraft from priestcraft. The divorce he advocates between politics and morality is meant to achieve this goal. Appropriately enough, readers of *The Prince* in the twentieth century spoke of "the autonomy of politics (from morality)" to describe this new sense of virtue. The expression is a good one since it refers to the two crucial innovations within Machiavelli's political thought: first, the idea that the state operates according to its own rules, which are not, per se, moral (by which I mean: according to natural law) but that must be respected if a state is to be acquired and maintained. Second, the one who has such state must at times act outside established morality and religion.

This is why Machiavelli begins Chapter 15 by proclaiming he will "depart from the order of others," namely, from what previous mirrors of princes recommended, because he is "after the effectual truth of the thing rather than the imagination of it" (chapter 15, p.87). He then explicitly specifies in what sense he departs from previous views: "For there is such a distance from how one lives to how one ought to live that he who abandons what is done for what ought to be done learns what will ruin him rather than what will save him, since a man who would wish to make a career of being good in every detail must come to ruin among so many that are not good. Hence it is necessary for a prince, if he wishes to maintain himself, to learn to be able to be not good, and to use this faculty and not to use it according to necessity" (chapter 15, p.87). Machiavelli abandons the teachings of natural law on the basis of necessity, and the necessity confronting every new prince is the fact that men are not "good." As Hobbes will say, man is a wolf to man. Given this necessity, the new prince has to learn to be "not good" and fight off the wolves without relying on a good shepherd to intervene and provide shelter. Machiavelli does not hide the fact that he is teaching how not to be good. So there is no surprise at all that *The Prince* quickly became synonymous with "Machiavellism" and shorthand for the idea that the end justifies the means.

But what is more surprising is the almost immediate popularity of this "evil" teaching. It was as if *The Prince* generated an enormous, collective sigh of relief, as if its author single-handedly liberated humankind from the unbearable weight exerted by the Platonic, and later Christian, claim that only one truly "good" form of life exists. Machiavelli's "evil" teaching boils down to this: we no longer have to be "good" (in the philosophical sense of moral virtues) to live in society with others; we can live with others and pursue our passions and desires, as long as we assure each other that all have the same liberty to pursue their own passions and desires. This mutual reassurance is based on a legitimate, that is a mutually consented, use of coercion on the part of the state.

Since Cicero's time, the "mirror of princes" worked through a list of virtues that the prince had to imitate in order to meet the favor of their subjects and retain the state. For Cicero there are four main "philosophical" virtues: wisdom (to perceive the absolute truth), justice (to give each their own), courage (to uphold what is just even if when unpleasant to ourselves), and temperance (to maintain one's passions under the control of reason).[45] These virtues are "philosophical" in the sense that they depend on the knowledge of a rational natural order (objective truth) and also that they apply even independently of social or political context. Additionally, Cicero adds three strictly "political" virtues essential for anyone who lives in a political community with others, and especially for whoever is charged with ruling these communities: keeping faith, liberality, and beneficence.[46]

When Machiavelli recalls the list of moral virtues in Chapter 15, he jumps directly to the "political" virtues, ignoring the "philosophical" ones. The reason for this appears only later in the text, when Machiavelli discusses what a natural order is, or whether there is one. For Machiavelli the space of politics is a space of appearance to others; it is a space of judgment and opinion, of interpretation, and not of objective truth. Objective truth is what philosophers and scientists think they attain and grasp; it is the essence of things, hidden from most of us unless we happen to be superior logicians, mathematicians, and metaphysicians. But politics is essentially concerned with how one appears to others, what opinion others have of one. Politics is the place where human beings seek out glory and greatness, which are rooted in opinion or reputation, not in objective truth, in appearance and not in essence. "For the masses are always captivated by appearances, and by the outcome of the thing," writes Machiavelli, "and in the world there are only the masses, and the few have no standing when the many have someone to support them" (chapter 19, p.96). Your two or three close friends may believe that you are a "great" person, endowed with all possible virtues, but if the rest of your classmates or office-workers ignore you, or find you contemptible, then you have neither glory nor greatness. To do that, you must engage in an activity everyone can behold; you must step on the stage of the world; you must seek to acquire state. The minute you do that, you take on a "persona" or "character" independent of essence, unencumbered by who you "really are." You have entered a conflictual space where your friends as much as your enemies only care about your "reputation."

Machiavelli rehearses the classical list of political virtues and their antonyms in order to dedicate a chapter to the discussion of each of them: a prince can be either liberal or a miser (Chapter 16); either compassionate (merciful) or cruel (Chapter 17); either faithful (honest) or a breaker of faith (Chapter 18); either timid or fierce (Chapter 19); either religious or unbelieving (Chapter 21). Machiavelli's innovative claim is that these virtues only "appear" to benefit a prince, while "in reality" they lead to ruin, and whereas "something else that will appear a vice, if adopted, will result in his security and well-being" (chapter 15, p.88). Additionally, he argues that a prince, since he or she cannot "be" virtuous in reality, must carefully "pretend" to be virtuous, giving outward signs of virtue while keeping him or herself free to be "not good." In other words, Machiavelli explicitly contradicts Cicero and Plato, who claim that "Socrates declared splendidly, the nearest path to glory … is to behave in such a way that one is what one wishes to be thought. For men who think that they can secure for themselves unshakeable glory by pretence and empty show, by dissembling in speech and countenance, are wildly mistaken … pretence can never endure."[47] Where classical political philosophy argued that a statesman must really be what he wishes others to see him as (so honesty is the mark of a true statesman), Machiavelli seems to argue that a statesman must never actually be how he or she is seen by others (so that the mark of statesman is now duplicity, that is, a form of hypocrisy). For the former, appearances must correspond to a stable reality; for the latter, the "effective truth" of politics is based on opinions, and these are inherently changeable, requiring a statesman to be willing and able to change his or her policies with the change of opinions. Let us see in more detail why it is necessary for all successful statesmen to be hypocrites.

Machiavelli began the chapter by announcing his interest in the reality, not the imagination, of power. What does he mean? First, he means that moral virtue in a leader is part of the imaginary, not of the real; it is a function of wishful thinking, not of actual relations of force. But whose imaginary, whose wishes, are we talking about? Clearly we are talking about the wishes of those on the receiving end of the prince's actions, namely, the subjects. This is indicated in the chapter's title: "On those things for which men and especially princes *are praised or criticized.*" It is clear why a state's subjects would hope their prince is a good person: if he or she is good, he or she will do them no harm. The people want their prince to be good out of self-interest. But the prince also knows that in politics interests are asserted not only through opinion but also through the clash of forces. The people, who want their ruler to be good and do no harm, see this ruler only through their own interest and might miss threats to the prince's security; indeed, they may even be unaware that they themselves are being taken advantage of by others in their society. To win something on behalf of the people might well require the prince make a "correct" use of cruelty and violence. Thus Machiavelli introduces here two criteria on which to measure the value of a leader's actions: does it appear the prince is doing what the people "wish" or "desire" from him or her (what is imagined)? And, is he or she also doing what is in their real "interest" (the effective truth)? As Machiavelli says in the above citation, the people only care about two things: appearances and outcomes.

By introducing the distinction between imagination and effective truth in politics, Machiavelli argues that any political action can be judged by those who suffer its effects according to two irreducible measures. Does the action match my wishes, or does it match my interests? As it happens, the distinction between doing what is in the interest of the principal and doing what the principal wishes is the fundamental distinction in the concept of political represen-tation.[48] A representative is always caught in a dilemma between fulfilling the promises made to electoral constituents (the wish-list of programs used to appeal to voters), and doing what is in the real interest of constituents (reneging on campaign promises—or making promises they know can never be fulfilled—not because these things are impossible, but because they must act in the interest of the people in the hopes of winning the next election).

In Machiavelli's time, modern representative democracy did not yet exist, but its rudiments were apparent in the increasing autonomy of representative bodies. This was a development occurring simul-taneously within the Church (referred to as Conciliarism) and in the new monarchies in, for instance, both England and France. Machiavelli praises the French Parliament's design to "beat down the great and favor the lesser folk" (ch.19, p.98). Looking further down this road than most of his contemporaries, he turns the new prince into a prince who depends on the favor of the people for the control of the state. As such, Machiavelli also recognized that this inevitably requires the new prince to become something no previous statesman had been, namely, a "representative" of the wishes and interests of his or her constituency. Machiavelli makes the prince an agent of his or her principal, the people. If the agent ends up harming the principal, he or she shall incur its "hatred"; hatred here refers to the response of a people whose rulers have lost all representative function with respect to the electorate. Avoiding the people's hatred becomes the highest maxim of the new prince: "the best fortress there is is not to be hated by the people. For even if you have fortresses, if the people hold you in hatred, the fortresses do not save you" (chapter 20, p.108).

We can now explain what kind of "duplicity" or "hypocrisy" Machiavelli requires of his new prince; it is a duplicity congenial to the political space of representation as a space of appearances, where the appearance of actor is the object of fabrication and manipulation, in short, where one's image or reputation is the object of an art. Making one's life into a work of art and fashioning the state into a work of art were, as we saw at the very start, characteristic features of Renaissance thought. Thus Machiavelli's *arte dello stato* is not only concerned with the "art" of exerting violence in order to create state, but also with the "art" of representing its leader. Politics is a question of representing yourself by making an image, a public "persona," a mask corresponding to the wishes of others while also granting you a degree of autonomy to act in ways contrary to this image, and in ways that they would judge to be "not good."

The apparent immorality of Machiavelli's political thinking is inseparable from the relativism of modern representative democracy. People elect a representative because, say, they desire lower taxes, or, another year, they may respond to promises of more job-creation, etc. Once in office, the politician becomes aware of the fact that lowering taxes as promised will hurt the very people she made the promise to. Should she stick to the wishes of the electorate, knowing that this will hurt their interests, or should she break her campaign promise and go against their wishes knowing she did something good for them, despite appearing to be a liar and a hypocrite? This common example is appropriate here because Machiavelli himself brings up these kinds of cases dealing with the welfare of subjects, in order to illustrate why an "effective" government may have to do things its principal may judge to be "not good." In his overturning of the classical catalogue of virtues, Machiavelli is anticipating a point that Mandeville and Adam Smith will make later when considering the way in which political economy functions, arguing that public virtues can be pursued by means of private vices. Analogously, in the case of the state, public vices, that is, vices of the prince—for instance, letting the state incur debt in order to buoy workers in a struggling economy by financing employment—may lead to private virtues, that is, advantages accruing to subjects.

The interplay between politics and economics runs through Machiavelli's new approach to princely virtues like a red thread. Thus, in Chapter 16 Machiavelli discusses whether a prince should be "liberal" in order to win friends and glory, as Cicero and Seneca had counseled. Machiavelli knows that the young Medici would-be prince to whom he dedicates his book comes from a family known for its "liberality" as masters of the art of patronage, spending liberally on their friends. If a prince depends on the friendship of other nobles, then liberality is crucial. But what do you get for friends who already "have everything"? Clearly, you need to spend lavishly and recklessly, as if money were of no concern to you, when in reality it is your sole concern. Since time immemorial, nobility of character has been measured by one's sacrifice and generosity, always involved in a gift economy of one-upmanship. This is what anthropologists call "potlatch." But Machiavelli identifies a problem with this anti-economic logic of the nobility: if the prince acquires the noble quality of liberality, soon he has little to give away, and must take from his people: "so that always a prince of this kind will consume all of his means. ... And he will be required in the end, if he wishes to maintain the name of a liberal man, to burden his people extraordinarily, to tax heavily, and do all those things that can be done to get money. This will begin to make him hateful to his subjects. ... So that, by means of this liberality of his, since he has offended the many and rewarded the few, he feels every new hardship, and with any new danger he is imperiled" (chapter 16, p.88). The "revaluation of all values" (Nietzsche) which Machiavelli recommends, in which what was a virtue now becomes a vice and what was a vice now turns into a virtue, depends entirely on the assumption that what is good for the nobility is bad for the people, and vice versa. One can even say something more radical: it is impossible for the new prince to ally him or herself with the people, and thus to found a democratic state, unless he or she starts from the relativity of all moral values. The belief in "one" authentic catalogue of virtues is only functional to an aristocratic government.

Machiavelli counsels the new prince not to worry that his or her economic prudence makes him or her "incur the infamy of the miser" among the people. What counts for the people is always the "effective truth," the "fact" that the prince is not stealing from them: "he must encourage his citizens to be able quietly to practice their trades, in commerce, in agriculture and in every other human occupation, so that one man is not afraid to improve his properties for fear they will be taken away from him, and another is not afraid to open a business for fear of taxes" (chapter 21, p.111). Machiavelli likes to use the expression, "when the deed accuses him, the effect excuses him" (D, I, 9, p.29). This formula is always applied to an "extraordinary" or exceptional action that falls outside the normal moral standards. Such an exceptional action, furthermore, must respond to a "necessity" of statecraft; and, lastly, the immoral action will be "excused" only if it benefits the people. Of course, things look different from the perspective of the nobles: for them, everything is in the name. If one brings dishonor or disgrace to one's name, then one is lost. That is why the safest course for the noble man is to be "virtuous." So thinks the aristocrat. Not so ordinary folk: they can distinguish between the name and the thing itself, and eventually they will re-name the miserly prince "liberal," not because she gives generously, but because she does not take from them unnecessarily. Just like with armies of one's own, so too with the friendship of the people: it is not for sale.

Machiavelli then moves on, in Chapter 17, to discuss the virtue of compassion or mercy and the vice of cruelty as a way to approach the fundamental question of whether it is better to be loved or feared by one's subjects. Cicero and Seneca both adamantly sided with the need for a statesman to be merciful with his subjects in order to win their approval or love. Machiavelli has another example in mind: he was witness to another Caesar, Cesare Borgia, with a reputation for cruelty (toward the landed nobility), but "that cruelty of his restored Romagna, unified it, and led it back to peace and faith" (chapter 17, p.90). By contrast, Machiavelli recalls how the "merciful" Florentine Republic for which he worked, fearing the rebellion of its subject cities, maintained its compassionate reputation by refusing to intervene in a civil war in one of its subject cities, thus causing enormous loss of human life. More recently, we see a similar logic at work in the inaction of the U.S. government faced with the genocide in Rwanda; or when Dutch United Nations troops, on the grounds that their mandate was "peacekeeping" and not killing rogue militias, stood idly by while pro-Serbian militias committed ethnic cleansing against Muslim Bosnians. "A prince, therefore, must not care about the infamy of cruelty in keeping his subjects united and faithful" (chapter 17, p.91) because showing compassion to those who plunder and kill the people (namely, the nobles) harms far more individuals than being cruel to a few nobles.

But cruel actions, even if directed at nobles, will make the prince feared and not loved, so the question remains, which is the better of the two? More specifically, does fear or love win the people over to the prince? Cicero's opinion is clear: "But there is nothing at all more suited to protecting and retaining influence than to be loved, and nothing less suited than to be feared."[49] Machiavelli defends the opposite position: given the choice, fear is better than love in keeping subjects faithful to the prince: "Men have less fear of offending one who makes himself loved than one who makes himself feared, since love is held in place by a bond of obligation which, because men are wretched, is broken at every opportunity for utility to oneself, but fear is held in place by a fear of punishment that never abandons you" (chapter 17, p.91). The key word here is "utility," or profit: it is a far stronger motive than love. Machiavelli's pessimistic anthropology conceives of human beings as utility maximizers, and this applies to love as to any other activity. If a marriage is not providing sufficient "utilities" for the couple, no matter how much they may love each other, the marriage will not last; conversely, if there is no love lost between the couple, but the marriage remains useful to both, then it will continue.

Plato's and Cicero's idea that the morally honest and the useful are never at odds collapses once human agency is analysed in terms of opinion, interest, and utility. Utility is generated through competition and not collaboration with others. Plato and Cicero believed that one's advantage depends on the solidarity of others. On this assumption, what is useful to one cannot be contrary to what is morally right or honest, because otherwise one could not generate the necessary solidarity. Machiavelli, instead, knows that one's advantage depends on competition with others. On this assumption, what is useful to one is often in tension with what is morally right or honest. One will try to exploit the solidarity of others while escaping its obligations. In order to avoid this "free-rider" dilemma, the alliance between the state and the people must be based on more than words and promises, namely, on the threat of punishment for breaking one's word. Hobbes later adopts this lesson from Machiavelli, arguing that the contract between citizens is viable because the state is exempt from such an agreement in order to maintain its monopoly on the use of violence in the service of guaranteeing that all other citizens follow the common rules or face the consequences levied by the sovereign state.

Cruelty in punishing misdeeds generates fear, but Machiavelli argues that it need not lead to hatred as long as the prince "abstains from the property of his citizens and his subjects, and from their women. And if he must proceed against someone's life, he should do it when there is appropriate justification and manifest cause" (chapter 17, p.92). The reasoning is always the same: the prince needs to secure his or her alliance with the people against the nobles; the key is to be feared by the nobles and not hated by the people. The interests of the people, namely, the security of their possessions and the establishment of the rule of law, is far more important to them than the fact that their ruler employs cruelty in achieving these ends.

The argument against avoiding the hatred of the people comes to a climax in Chapter 18, where Machiavelli discusses whether a prince should keep his promises or break faith. This is a particularly tricky point: if all social bonds are the products of alliances between people, then of what utility can it be to break one's promises, to have no faith? The Roman political tradition and the monotheistic religions are united in placing the virtue of keeping faith (however this term if understood) as the highest moral virtue, the basis of everything else. Cicero argues that there is no conceivable "utility" to be gained by breaking one's word (in being dishonest) because everything of utility to us is a function of our sociability with others. Utility, according to Cicero, is the product of exchange and commerce with others, which depends on trust and keeping promises, on contracts; should we be found wanting in faith, then no one will want to exchange anything with us anymore. Machiavelli objects to this logic. He is wary of the demand that promises be kept even when it is no longer in our interest to do so: Why should I not lie to the deranged man knocking at my door looking to kill someone hiding in my house? Why should poor countries adhere to international trade pacts that systematically plunder their wealth? Why should I keep faith with a citizen or a prince who turns out to be a wolf in sheep's clothing?

In order to address this fundamental problem, Machiavelli cites Cicero's discussion of conflict, only to invert his evaluation. Cicero writes, "There are two types of conflict: one proceeds by debate, the other by force. Since the former is the proper concern of a man, but the latter of beasts, one should only resort to the latter if one may not employ the former".[50] Cicero associates the beast in man with the source of injustice: "deceit seems to belong to a little fox, force to a lion. Both of them seem most alien to a human being; but deceit deserves a greater hatred. And out of all injustice, nothing deserves punishment more than that of men who, just at the time when they are most betraying trust, act in such a way that they might appear to be good men."[51] Machiavelli, on the other hand, argues that when men act like wolves there is no sense in fighting them without force, in trying to persuade them to change their ways. On the contrary, against wolves the prince must make use of both the guile of the fox and the brute force of the lion: the lion needs the fox in order to avoid the subtle traps other competitors set up for him, while the fox needs the lion to fend off the wolves. "Therefore a prudent lord cannot, nor should he, observe faith when such observance turns against himself. ... And if men were all good, this precept would not be good; but because they are wicked, and they would not observe faith for you, you too do not have to observe it for them" (chapter 18, p.94).

But Machiavelli's revaluation of the animal nature of humans is not simply a function of his belief that only force can match force, that only power can check oppression. Animal life represents an economy of violence. The animal symbolizes an artful, measured use of violence; animals kill out of necessity; their cruelty is well-used. Anticipating Nietzsche, Machiavelli was one of the few to appreciate the Dionysian basis of Greek culture in understanding the myth of Achilles' (the greatest Greek prince and warrior) education by Chiron, a centaur, half-man half-horse, to mean "that it is necessary for a prince to know how to use one and the other nature; and the one without the other does not endure" (chapter 18, p.94).

As discussed above, every state has to confront two permanent sources of conflict. One is internal, centered on the struggle between the privileged few and the exploited and oppressed many. The other is external, arising from the permanent temptation for states to enlarge their territories and spheres of influence at the expense of other states. Machiavelli is the first political thinker not only to understand that foreign policy is an essential part of politics, but also to discover that no state lasts in time unless it expands; it is in the very dynamic of the (nation-)state to seek to expand into an empire and dominate its neighbors. If a state wants to maintain its freedom and self-dependence, while avoiding becoming dependent on other states, then it inevitably tends to expand into an "empire" or what today we could call a "superpower." This general law applies to republics as much as to principalities, the United States of America being a prime example of an imperial republic in our times.

But when a state begins to make the transition to empire, the nature of the army necessarily changes as the citizenry and military begin to divide themselves into separate constituencies with disparate interests. Citizens, for their part, want to enjoy the fruits of empire, such as peace and security, industry and culture, at home. The army, on the other hand, is motivated by the potential wealth procured in wars abroad, or, what is virtually the same, by the investments that flow into their coffers through preparation for war. Pretty soon these two constituencies clash, and statesmen must confront the perennial question of whether to favor "guns or butter": should they invest more in defense or in social security spending? Should they project a "fierce" image of themselves or a "timid" one? If one judges by the budgets of powerful states, it is clear as day that what Eisenhower called the "military industrial complex" is a heavyweight political player to be disregarded by politicians only at a high cost. This is the question that Machiavelli approaches in Chapter 19. Since it is a question that only makes sense once the state enters into an imperial dimension, Machiavelli tackles it by giving a long analysis of Roman emperors and how they fared when confronting this dilemma.

In the previous chapters Machiavelli has been hammering home the claim that princes fall from power when they incur the hatred of people. But, after rehearsing the point once more, in Chapter 19 he quickly moves to his real concern, addressing the second reason a prince loses power: inconsistency. Once a prince is "believed to be changeable, light, effeminate, pusillanimous, irresolute"—in the terminology of today's pundits, they "flip-flop" on the issues—they risk the contempt of both the citizenry and military (chapter 19, p.96). The real question here is who is more bothered by the statesman's flip-flopping: the people or the military? Machiavelli does not hesitate to answer that a prince's "timidity" produces a reaction of contempt in the military (and in any other citizen who identifies with the interests of the military). Obviously, a "timid" or "pusillanimous" leader is disinclined toward military adventures, thus curtailing the source of utility for the military-industrial complex (which also affects a considerable chunk of the citizenry).

This fact places the prince in an untenable position, since what is required to avoid the contempt of an imperial military, characterized by "avarice and cruelty," is entirely different from what it takes to be feared by the people: "for the people loved quiet, and for this reason they loved modest princes; and the soldiers loved the prince of military virtue, and that he should be insolent, cruel and rapacious" (chapter 19, p.99). Roman emperors, according to Machiavelli, had to choose between upholding peace and justice at home or cranking up the war machine abroad. This dilemma has no simple solution, because those emperors who tried to slow down the military were killed by their own soldiers, while those princes who sought an alliance with the army ended up harming the people and incurring their hatred, thus eventually also falling into ruin.

The two exceptions are Marcus Aurelius, the philosopher-emperor, who was moderate without ever incurring the contempt of the army; and Severus, who was able to keep the state despite not sparing "any kind of injury that could be committed against the people" because "those virtues of his made him so marvelous in the sight of the soldiers and the people and the latter remained somehow stupefied and astonished, and the former reverent and satisfied" (chapter 19, p.101). Severus is "a most ferocious lion and a most clever fox," except that he used his *virtù* against the people and always favored the military. What are the reasons why these two emperors did not fall? Here Machiavelli returns to the categories he began the book with and relies on the distinction between a hereditary prince and a new one. Marcus Aurelius was a hereditary prince: he did not depend on the favor of the military to reach power, so the military did not feel he owed them any special treatment. But Severus was a "new prince" who desperately needed the support of the military to confront both the nobles and the people in order to acquire the state, and for that reason he sided with the military against the people. And yet he was not hated by the people because he kept them always "stupefied and astonished" at his evil deeds, while keeping the military "reverent and satisfied."

What lesson is the new prince supposed to draw from this analysis? Strangely enough for him, Machiavelli comes up with a compromise: "he must choose from Severus those parts that are necessary to found his state, and from Marcus those that are appropriate and glorious for preserving a state that is already established and firm" (chapter 19, p.104). Depending on the situation the prince finds him or herself in, whether it is the moment of acquisition of state or the moment of maintaining state, he or she must adopt a different set of virtues, a different personality.

But this returns us to a fundamental question raised by the analysis of virtue, namely, the question of the mask or persona of the prince. Machiavelli's point is that virtue is a question of image. Depending on the situation, the prince must appear to be X when in reality he is Y, etc. The *virtù* of the new prince, then, lies in being "a great pretender and dissembler, and men are so very simple, and they so well obey present necessities, that he who deceives will always find someone who will allow himself to be deceived" (chapter 18, p.94). Given the relativity of moral virtue as the basic condition of politics, Machiavelli concludes that political *virtù*, the quality that allows the prince to acquire and keep state, is a detachment from any fixed character or quality, leading some interpreters to speak of the prince as a "man without qualities," to borrow the title of Musil's novel.[52]

In Chapters 18 and 21 Machiavelli argues that the virtue the new prince most needs to feign is "religion." He gives the example of Ferdinand the Catholic: "a certain prince of present times,

whom it is best not to name, never preaches anything but peace
and faith, and he is a great enemy of both; and if he had observed
both, either his reputation or his state would have been taken
from him" (chapter 18, p.96). Ferdinand's specialty was justifying
his expansive policies by appealing to religious motivations; in
short, Ferdinand carried out his project of state-building through
religious wars: "so as to be able to undertake greater campaigns,
ever making use of religion, he resorted to an act of pious cruelty
by chasing the Marranos [Jews and Muslims who fled persecution,
some of whom converted to Christianity but maintained their faith
in their old religion] from his kingdom and despoiling them: nor
could this example be more wretched or more rare. ... And so he
has always done and ordered great things, which have always kept
the spirits of his subjects suspended and wondering and occupied
with their outcome" (chapter 21, p.109). Ferdinand is therefore a
most Catholic prince and at the same time a most "Machiavellian"
one. What is Machiavelli trying to insinuate through this example?
He seems to think that the state should adopt religion for its own
purposes, and not contrariwise. Interestingly enough, the reception
of *The Prince* by the doctrine of "reason of state" carries on both
possibilities at once. Second, Machiavelli prepares the ground for
the last chapter of the book, dedicated to divine providence, where
he returns to the discussion of ecclesiastical principalities and the
priority of war, asking: is it the case that God and war are opposed?
Or is there another conception of divine providence, in which God
and conquest of state are compatible? Third, Machiavelli clearly
condemns Ferdinand's expulsion of the Jews as well as his crusade
against Muslims as "wretched." Is there here another indication,
perhaps, that Machiavelli's idea of divine providence will not be
drawn from the Catholic conception of God's actions in history,
but from the alternative conceptions found in Judaism and Islam?

STUDY QUESTIONS

1 Under what social conditions could politics be modeled exclusively on
   moral criteria? Are these conditions likely to obtain?
2 Should politicians always do what their constituencies ask them to do?
3 Is there a fundamental distinction, morally speaking, between acting
   in the private sphere and acting in the public sphere?

CHAPTER EIGHT

Disarming fortune and the arming of heaven

Chapters 24–26

The concluding section of *The Prince* contains the most philosophical chapter of the entire text (Chapter 25, dedicated to chance) and the most puzzling (Chapter 26, dedicated to providence). Machiavelli states the central problem of this section in Chapter 24. Before the French king made the fateful decision to invade Italy, causing the series of unpredictable events that forced Machiavelli out of his job—landing him at his desk composing *The Prince*—the republics and principalities in Italy were more or less stable. The invasion shattered this balance of power, with states changing hands at a worrisome and puzzling rate as a consequence. Some, like Savonarola, saw in this political chaos the hand of God: a divine punishment to princes for their evil deeds. Others, among them most philosophers and humanists, began to think there was no way to counteract the power of chance (*fortuna*) in human affairs.

In practical terms, these beliefs in the supremacy of God and chance over human affairs excluded "science" as a guide for acquiring and holding state; power and glory are bestowed by God or chance (which, since Roman times, was personified by the goddess Fortuna) and either force can take them away at will. Both God and chance lie beyond the reach of human reason and calculation. The focus on the power of God and of chance meant an inherent limit to human virtue and strength because human success requires the external help of some superior force. Machiavelli was keenly aware that these beliefs about God and chance threatened his whole project. If God rules everything, then human self-assertion, the very idea of depending on one's wits and strength, is blasphemous and, more to the point, entirely useless. If the *virtù* of the new prince is no match for the power of *Fortuna*, what is the point of writing *The Prince*? Its newly discovered technique, its entire *arte dello stato*, would have no more chance to succeed than no technique whatsoever. Machiavelli had to challenge both these beliefs or see the entire scientific edifice of his treatise crumble to the ground. Unless he could propose an alternative idea of God and of chance, his prince's state would be built on mud.

That is why Machiavelli argues that "these princes of ours, who were in their principalities for many years, ought not to accuse fortune for having lost them, but their own laziness" (chapter 24, p.116). The crucial word is "laziness" (*ignavia*, literally, lacking in will-power, in *virtù*). To appeal to the inscrutability of God's will or to the mythical power of *Fortuna* to excuse one's failures is a symptom of intellectual and practical laziness; human beings "give" *Fortuna* her power through their lack in *virtù*. Machiavelli's general belief is that Christian morality had made human beings "lazy" by taking away the need for self-reliance. Still, does this mean that Machiavelli wants to substitute the omnipotence of Man for the power of God or chance?[53]

If we look back to Chapter 7, where Machiavelli analyses the rise and fall of his new ideal prince, we see that he hesitates as to the causes of Cesare Borgia's downfall. At first, Machiavelli chalks it up to the bad luck that Cesare became seriously ill just as his powerful father died; but, at the end of the chapter, Machiavelli claims that Cesare made a "poor choice" in helping bring his arch-enemy Julius II to power. In any case, no one can accuse Cesare of "laziness." And yet he was brought down by chance. Something similar can be said about Machiavelli's attitude toward divine providence. Despite not believing in anything that the Church teaches about the calendar of human salvation, Machiavelli remains unwilling to give up on the idea of a special providence. So, even as he challenges the prevalent beliefs about God and chance, Machiavelli does not want to place the human being at the center of the universe (and how could he want this after arguing that humans are living beings just like any other animal, and not the crown of Creation). Rather, we shall see that for him it is far more a question of how to turn the favor of God or chance to one's benefit.

Machiavelli describes contemporary princes as lazy because "they never during quiet times thought that the times could change. ... Then, when adverse times did come, they decided to flee, not to defend themselves" (chapter 24, p.116). The princes of Machiavelli's time made no contingency plans; it was as if their misconception of the power of chance made planning futile. The great philosophical contribution of *The Prince* is to provide a new conception of contingency and chance that inspires and motivates human activity rather than passivity. Today we are so in tune with Machiavelli's conception of chance that we have contingency plans for nearly every aspect of life. We call this "insurance." As anyone who has ever invested in the stock market knows, anything is possible, anything can happen. Money is made in the stock market not by betting on what is going to happen (as if one is playing the roulette), but by betting on our collective ignorance of what is going to happen. This means that one spreads the risk as much as possible; one "insures" one's bets by betting against them and against oneself, and so on. This active approach toward uncertainty is the quintessence of what Machiavelli teaches the new prince. If the new princes want to keep their states, then they had better spread their risk by arming their people; if they want to "defend" themselves, then they must bet on the people (the traditional enemies of kings and princes) and against the nobles (the traditional friends of kings and princes). If the new princes want to beat the odds, then they must appear to do what is expected of them while actually doing exactly the opposite. That's all well and good, but why will it work? What is chance, and who is God? And what do both have to do with the new-found importance of the people in politics?

Machiavelli begins his treatment of chance or fortune by voicing the widespread opinion "that the things of the world are governed by fortune and by God, that men, with their prudence, cannot correct them. ... that there would be no point in sweating much in the things of this world, but let themselves be governed by chance" (chapter 25, p. 116). Plato's *Laws*, whose recent translation into Latin was avidly read by Machiavelli's contemporaries as a blueprint of the ideal republic, advances a similar view that only "god—and together with god, chance and opportunity—pilots all human things."[54] This coordination of God and chance in guiding the course of human affairs is better known as "divine providence." Plato goes on to argue that for a wise legislator to produce a brand new code of moral and political laws for a city he requires a "tyrannized city ... and let the tyrant be young, possessed of an able memory, a good learner, courageous and magnificent by nature."[55] Obviously, it is much easier to bring laws to an enslaved people than to a people who already are capable of giving themselves the laws they want. But this happy match between the tyrant and the legislator (in other words, the philosopher) can only be the fruit of a rare coincidence: "if this should happen, then the god has done almost all the things that he does when he wants some city to fare especially well."[56] For philosophers to rule, divine providence must exist.

Plato gives so much power to chance only in order to show that average human beings cannot govern themselves. Because chance is unbeatable, human beings need a wise founder to give them a divine code of laws to obey scrupulously, one that stands above politics, protecting human beings from the risks of political conflict and discord. For Plato, giving laws to a city counts as "the most perfect of all tests of manly virtue."[57] Thus, with this concept of divine providence, Plato is the first to introduce the idea that "manly virtue" and chance can be reconciled in a political project that founds an unchangeable system of law and order.

Introduced by Plato, the reconciliation between "virtue" (*virtus*) and "chance" (*fortuna*) becomes the fundamental motif of political thought in the West all the way up to Machiavelli. With Polybius, the Greek historian of the Roman Empire, this idea enters into Roman political thought; through Boethius, it dominates much of Christian political thought. Ficino is one of the last great exponents of this Platonic idea of providence.

Giovanni Rucellai—the Florentine aristocrat and banker who was a close ally of Cosimo de' Medici—once asked Ficino in a letter whether "human reason and practical cleverness can do something against the contingencies of Fate or Fortuna." Ficino answers that "it is good to combat *fortuna* with the weapons of prudence, patience and magnanimity. Better still is to flee such a war from which very few come out victorious and those few with intellectual effort and extreme exertion. The best of all is to make peace with her by conforming our will with hers and willingly go where she points to so that she will not drag us there by force. We will do all this if in us there is harmony between patience, wisdom, and will. Finis. Amen."[58] Following the Platonic respect for chance, Ficino recommends disengaging from the conflict between virtue and chance (*fortuna*) at the level of human action. Since chance is that aspect of God's plan that we do not know, and thus appears to us as irrational, the attempt to change the course of affairs determined by chance amounts to an act of impiety pitting the individual against the divinely established, "fatal and legal" order of things.

Giovanni Rucellai followed Ficino's advice to prudently adapt one's virtue to the ways of *fortuna* to the letter. Giovanni apparently conceived of the marriage between his son, Bernardo, and Lorenzo the Magnificent's sister, Nannina, as a successful adaptation to *fortuna*. Bernardo Rucellai was not only the leader of the aristocratic faction fighting against Savonarola's Republic, but an accomplished humanist, a student of Roman history, who opened his gardens to the on-going philosophical discussions of the Florentine élites. Machiavelli was eventually invited and it was here that he delivered his lectures on Livy. A print from this period represents Bernardo's alliance with the Medici family depicting him naked, in the position of a mast, holding up the sails of a boat steered by Nannina de' Medici. The inscription reads: "I let myself be carried by *fortuna* hoping that in the end the outcome will be good."[59] This document testifies to the longstanding decision by the Rucellai banking family to tie itself to the political fortunes of the Medici family, with Nannina representing the mythical Fortuna herself. Just like Plato's appreciation of chance grows out of a specific attempt to bring about an absolute government of laws through tyranny, Ficino's embrace of *fortuna* over political craft (*virtù*) expresses the ideological reality of Renaissance Florence's passive or contemplative attitude toward Fortuna and the active support for an aristocratic, if not tyrannical, understanding of politics (embodied by the Medici rule over Florence).

What Machiavelli thinks of all this is easily discerned if one jumps to the infamous conclusion of Chapter 25: "fortune is a lady, and it is necessary, if one wants to hold her down, to beat her and dash her" (chapter 25, p.119). The idea of reconciling oneself to *fortuna* is gone, and Bernardo Rucellai's political practice of weaving together the alliance between Medici and other noble families, leaving out of power the common people, is ridiculed.

But Machiavelli must bring the reader to this shocking conclusion. So he begins by admitting he often feels "inclined" to adapt a fatalistic position, but that he resists this conclusion because otherwise "free will" would be "eliminated." Instead, he presents another hypothesis, "that fortune is the arbiter of half of our actions, but that she indeed allows us to govern the other half of them" (chapter 25, p.117). Without mentioning his name, Machiavelli here refers to Aristotle's defense of free choice and against the deterministic "Lazy" or "Idle Argument" (*argos logos, ratio ignava*) first introduced in *De Interpretatione* IX. Machiavelli's use of the term "laziness" (*ignavia*) in Chapter 24 directly indicates his awareness of the general outlines of the great debates on determinism, choice, and contingency in classical philosophy, as they emerged with renewed vigor in his own times.[60]

We generally accept that whatever is past and true is necessary; in other words, the past is irrevocable. The determinists ask why this should be any different with respect to the future. We tend to think the future is changeable because we believe that possibilities exist in an unrealized state, that is, that something exists (namely, the possible) which is not *yet* true (real, actual) and might *never* be true (realized, actualized). For the determinists, only what is real exists, so what we call "possible" is only a name for what is true or will be true since all times. That means that the necessity that applies to the past also applies to the future. I can no more change what will happen tomorrow than I can will that Hitler had never been born. From this deterministic argument follows the so-called Lazy Argument: if everything that happens is necessary then there is no need to deliberate or choose between options in the mistaken belief that if one does such and such it will change the course of future events.

Aristotle famously responds that it is evident certain events are "up to us": if I choose to get up from this chair, then my getting up will come to happen; if I choose against it, then it will not come to happen. Human deliberation and choice, the combination Aristotle names "prudence," is therefore an active force in the world. Before I actually decide to get up, my getting up from the chair is neither true nor false, but simply possible, a future contingency. For

Aristotle human deliberation depends on the independent existence of future contingents. The refutation of determinism requires the contingent character of future events, since without this it would make no sense to deliberate or make choices on what to do; in turn, this contingency depends on the natural, not divine, existence of chance. For Aristotle, in fact, God does not control everything that happens: contingent things are too insignificant for Him to contemplate. Rather it is precisely the existence of contingencies that makes human prudence and freedom possible. Thus, Machiavelli's conjecture that *fortuna* governs "about half" of human actions and leaves "up to us" the government of the other half, basically echoes the Aristotelian view.

From the point of view of prudence, the power of chance looks like a river whose force can be channeled by human actions: "She [Fortuna] shows her power where *virtù* is not prepared to resist her; and she turns her rushing current here where she knows that embankments and dikes have not been made to hold her" (chapter 25, p.117). With this "optimistic" thesis, Machiavelli overturns, at least partially, the Idle Argument in favor of the "active" resistance to *fortuna* posed by "orderly virtù."

Machiavelli's image of Fortuna as a river to be controlled by human *virtù* is not original.[61] Our old friend Bernardo Rucellai's *De Bello Italico* contains the image of the river that needs to be contained in a prudent fashion; and the same image is rehearsed by the humanist Pontano, in a famous "mirror of princes" written some years before Machiavelli's own book. In Pontano and Rucellai the "prudent" individual keeps up with the changes of the times thanks to the crucial quality of versatility (*versatilitas*), the capacity to change modes of proceeding in response to changing circumstances. Even Machiavelli had previously toyed with this idea: in Chapter 18 he writes that a prince "needs to have a spirit disposed to change as the winds of fortune and the variation of things command him" (chapter 18, p.95).

But here, halfway through Chapter 25, he suddenly changes course, starting, instead, to argue as if he's swimming against the current of *Fortuna*. Going back to an account of chance which he first developed in a letter known as the *Ghiribizzi al Soderino* from 1506, he proposes to think of fortune as a function of an encounter (*riscontro*) between actions and circumstances which draws upon Lucretius' belief that all things in the world depend on unforeseeable encounters between atoms which have swerved off their linear courses. "I believe, too, that the man who conforms [*riscontra*] his way of proceeding to the quality of the times is happy, and similarly that he whose proceedings the times disagree with is unhappy [*discordano e' tempi*]" (chapter 25, p.117).

According to this explanation, individuals proceed toward their common goals in different ways and with different means. In fact, contrary ways and means can lead equally to the same result, just as similar ways can lead to contrary results. What decides the outcome of a certain action is the match (or lack thereof) between the "quality of the times" (*qualità de' tempi*) and the ways of proceeding, the "quality of the action." Accounting for human action in this way undercuts the very premises of a theory of prudence because it rejects the idea that prudential deliberation about the means can determine the achievement of the desired end.

The circumstances of human action, the "quality of the times," favor different means at different times, allowing for a variety of ways of acting to succeed and continue their development. Whereas the Aristotelian theory of prudence favors those individuals who are endowed with practical wisdom, Machiavelli's theory of chance opens the possibility of a happy (or unhappy) outcome to all modes of action. Human ways of proceeding in the world are constituted by virtue of their adaptability to circumstances. The variety of human "habits" or "natures" is a consequence of a process of historical selection which is anti-teleological, in at least two senses: it is not because someone has a certain nature or virtue that they can better cope with the circumstances; on the contrary, it is the fact that certain actions cope with the circumstances that accounts for their becoming the functions or habits or natures which characterize that individual. In a second sense, the sphere of human action is anti-teleological because the necessity of coping with circumstances, or of "matching" the quality of one's actions with the qualities of the times, is itself historically variable in that it has no determinable final end: human nature is entirely given over to historical becoming.

Machiavelli's theory of the encounter in a Lucretian universe brings down, one after the other, all the pillars of the Aristotelian doctrine of prudence. It is only the encounter (*riscontro*) with the times and circumstances which determines the value of the means employed; the means are "good" (in the sense of adequate) if the encounter is favorable; they are "bad" otherwise. The implication is that the "good" varies with the times and according to situations; it cannot be determined prudentially, that is, ahead of time and in reference to a rule independent of the situation.

Furthermore, the variations of fortune depend on a change of circumstances that is not matched by a change in the course of action. "Nor is a man to be found who is so prudent that he knows how to accommodate himself to this: both because he cannot deviate from that toward which his nature inclines him, and, moreover, because when a man has always prospered by walking in one path, he cannot be persuaded to depart it ... although if he could change his nature with the times and with the circumstances, he would not change his fortune" (chapter 25, p.119). The virtue of "versatility" that humanists like Rucellai and Pontano saw as the primary quality of the prudent individual is thus impossible. No one is so wise as to always maintain good fortune by means of changing their nature every time the times change.

Some interpreters argue that Machiavelli concludes *The Prince* with this pessimistic picture of human nature, according to which our luck only changes due to our in-built limits, our incapacity to change our nature at will.[62] The mythical power of the goddess Fortuna is explained and demystified through an anthropological, naturalistic explanation. But if this is the case, then what is the point of Machiavelli's disrespect for chance? In reality, Machiavelli's "naturalism" boils down to the idea that human "nature" is completely a function of habits of action acquired thanks to the favor bestowed by circumstances on a given way of proceeding, that is, thanks to the adaptation of these ways to the times. Human "nature" for Machiavelli is therefore a function of custom; it is always "second" nature. If human "nature" is but a result of a certain pattern of adaptation between actions and circumstances, a result of an evolution, then it is also possible to conceive of a mode of action that breaks custom.

Machiavelli never says that the encounter (*riscontro*) between action and times has to be a harmonious correspondence between the two. Evolution does not exclude revolution: when *virtù* sets itself the goal of changing the times, rather than merely "corresponding" or "adapting" itself to the times, then *fortuna* is stripped of its status as sole cause of the change of times. Understood this way, Machiavelli's "pessimistic" theory of chance turns out to be a vehement attack on the reduction of action to behavior. Behavior is a reified type of predictable and controllable human activity based on pattern. Behavior is habitual action. This sort of activity is doomed to depend upon the favor or disfavor of the circumstances: behavior has the capacity to turn success into the cause of failure precisely because success strengthens the pattern, making it more entrenched and harder to break with, thereby rendering the human being under its sway more vulnerable to changes of circumstance.

As we have seen, Machiavelli's concludes his argument in Chapter 25 with a leap. Although the "quality of the times" is indifferent toward the modes of human action, now favoring one, then another of these, still "it is better to be impetuous than cautious" because "fortune is a lady" who wants someone "to hold her down, to beat her and to dash her." For this reason, *fortuna* will always favor those who do not respect her but are "more ferocious, and they command her with more audacity" (chapter 25, p.119). It turns out that "Lady Luck" desires a warrior more than a philosopher. We shall see in Chapter 26 that God also prefers a warrior to a philosopher.

The formula with which Machiavelli closes his discourse on *fortuna* is unprecedented in the history of political thought. No one before thought the conflict between virtue and fortune irreconcilable and certainly not of such dramatic proportions. But this is because they were caught up in the idea of prudence. They were convinced a divine mind predetermined the "match" between human action and its circumstances, allowing some human minds, in contact with God, to see beyond their situation (this capacity is called *pronoia, providentia*), thereby granting these superior human beings the ability to change their actions in accordance with the times (this capacity is properly called *phronesis, prudentia*). The fundamental presupposition of a theory of prudence is that the goal of human praxis is achieving a correspondence or reconciliation between action and times, between virtue and chance.

Machiavelli, instead, advances the idea that what the times call for, or favor, is precisely to act against the times. Indeed, audacity designates the quality of an action that goes "against the current" of the times, doing what is completely unexpected by breaking with longstanding habits. A call for audacity is always a call to change the current situation. The encounter between action and times is conceived as a coincidence of opposites, in the sense that what is "favored" by *fortuna*, what determines the concordance between action and the times, is precisely the war or conflict between them.

Machiavelli believes that human beings always find themselves in a situation not of their own choosing and which they cannot see beyond through wisdom, or some such connection to the divine mind. But he also believes that human beings are always capable of changing their situation: human action can transcend custom and habit. When an action breaks with the customary and innovates orders and laws, then it becomes a political action. It in this context that Machiavelli concludes it is absurd to "respect" chance. If the question is whether the times or circumstances allow for their change or not, then the answer can only be provided by taking one's chances with the action itself, pursued with audacity (*audacia*) and forcefulness (*impeto*). There is no sense in being "respectful" when the course of action at issue is revolutionary, precisely seeking to change the times. A gamble is a gamble, whether one is betting much or little. One cannot, in this sense, truly be respectful and at the same time a gambler. This is the second, more general meaning of Machiavelli's formula that *fortuna* is a woman who loves youth: chance loves those who take their chances, and conversely there is chance because there are those who take chances.

The heavens are armed

If *Fortuna* grants her favors more easily to those leaders who arm and fight with their people, what about God? The title of the last Chapter, "An exhortation to seize Italy, and to set her free from the barbarians," actually lays at the feet of the Medici dedicatee the task that Pope Julius II, known for his audacity, attempted and failed to accomplish. The civil prince must do what the Catholic Church never wanted to do, namely, unite Italy and make it unconquerable by foreign armies. Since the Church depended for its temporal power on keeping Italy divided and at the mercy of the "barbarians," Machiavelli's proto-nationalist project also entailed bringing about the end of the Church's temporal power. Additionally, in order to achieve this audacious enterprise, the civil prince would have to grab "absolute" power in order to found a new nation state. Machiavelli closes Chapter 25 in praise of audacious action for good reason: he is preparing the reader for his extremely audacious proposition in Chapter 26.

Given this context, it makes perfect sense for him, at the end of the book, to ask whether God would favor such audacity; to ask, would God be willing to see a new popular sovereign take the place of the Pope as His representative on earth? Once Machiavelli answers this question in the affirmative, which had never been asked nor answered in such blunt terms, all the great modern political thinkers rushed through the breach he opened. Hobbes, Spinoza, Rousseau, Kant, Hegel, Marx: all of them, in one form or another, had no qualms asserting that the march of popular sovereignty through history, the revolutionary conquest of monarchy and aristocracy by the power of the people, is the actual meaning of divine providence and the meaning of history.

The question of God's role in politics crops up repeatedly in Machiavelli's discourse, but it reaches its climax in the last Chapter. For many interpreters, Chapter 26 seems to contain two riddles. Why does Machiavelli appeal to divine providence in order to bolster the ambitions of the "new prince," when he advances "irreligious" theses in the rest of the book? Does he seriously mean what he says in the Chapter or is it merely a rhetorical flourish? The second riddle has to do with the "monarchic" airs taken by the new prince who is to unify Italy: how does this stand with his adoption throughout most of his writings of a staunchly pro-popular government stance? Does Machiavelli return to the old figures of divine providence and monarchy at the very end of a book that called both of these into question?[63] Or is there another way of understanding the unexpected appearance of divine monarchy in the last chapter of this book?

Let's begin by thinking about the way God favors some politics over others. This is not a new question for Machiavelli, since in his *Discourses on Livy* he discusses at length the essential role played by religion in the Roman Republic, thereby inaugurating the modern treatment of what is called "civil religion" (D, I, 11–15, pp.34–43). But Savonarola's preaching also brought to life for the Florentines another Republic that received the favor of the (true) God, namely, the Republic of the Hebrews. Here were two perfect case studies of God's role in politics that Machiavelli could oppose to the way the Christian Church conceived and taught, for more than a thousand years, God's supposed disdain for politics.

Machiavelli reasons as follows: both the Romans and the Jews were very religious peoples; they were also peoples who, for long stretches of their history, organized themselves politically so as to give power to the people rather than to kings; and, last but not least, they were also peoples who were constantly involved in warfare with other peoples. So, for Machiavelli, the obvious question is this: if the citizens of these two Republics, in the very practice of their political and military lives, sincerely believed that they were "imitating" God, and that God also believed this and granted them victory after victory, then who is this God? What sort of God favors the most ferocious and pitiless aspects of politics as illustrated by Roman historians and by the Hebrew Bible (for example: the constant pursuit of foreign conquest; the practices of decimation of their own populations; the necessity for their leaders to know when to break their promises and, at the same time, to cultivate their image as men of faith; and so on)?

Machiavelli's final theory of chance is characterized by a thoroughgoing naturalist or evolutionary perspective of human history. But now in Chapter 26 he raises his sights from the plane of man's natural history to the plane of man's sacred history: "Beyond this, see here the extraordinary things, without precedent, conducted by God: the sea has opened; a cloud has shown you the way, the stone has poured forth water; here the manna has rained down" (chapter 26, p.121). Is there a way to reconcile an evolutionary and naturalistic approach to human natural history with a providential one?

In Chapter 6, the opposition Machiavelli posits between the "armed prophet"—represented by Moses—and the "unarmed prophet"—represented by Savonarola—is clearly based on a distinction between the Jewish and the Christian conceptions of divine providence, which on many counts diverge from each other. If this is so, then maybe we should also apply this distinction to Machiavelli's treatment of providence in Chapter 26, as a consequence reading it in light of a Jewish rather than a Christian idea of divine providence. What difference does this make?

Medieval political thought was not only a Christian affair. Outside of the Christian mainstream, sometimes against the current, medieval Arabic and Jewish thinkers asked the question of what kind of Church-less "republic" God wished to establish through His philosophers/prophets/kings. From Spain and Portugal, through

France and Germany, this political thought trickles down to Italian humanist culture by way of several possible conduits, both known and yet to be discovered by future studies. Certainly the "Latin Averroism" of a Brunetto Latini, a Dante, and a Marsilius of Padua plays a significant role; but so too does the "Hebraic" Thomism of a Ptolemy of Lucca or a Savonarola; not to mention the syncretism of "Platonic" theology and Kabbalah in a Pico and a Ficino; and finally directly through the available translations into Latin of Alfarabi, Averroes, Maimonides, and, closer still to Machiavelli's Florence, Yohannan Alemanno and Isaac Abravanel. It is unclear how much from these sources reached Machiavelli, but there is no doubt that a great deal of this way of thinking about religion and politics would have found him an interested and creative receiver.

Christian providence depends on the postulate that, from all times, God has established the calendar of salvation (at whose center point stands the death and resurrection of Jesus Christ). It follows that nothing can be done to accelerate the return of the Messiah. From a Christian standpoint, the Messiah will not return *in* history, but only once history will be at its End. On the basis of this divine economy of salvation, the Roman Catholic Church is the only legitimate representative of God on earth; so long as the Catholic Church still stands, the End of History has not yet been reached.

A few centuries before Machiavelli, with a friar named Joachim of Fiore (1130–1202), this dispensational conception of Christian providence began its process of "secularization," pointing to a divine order *in* history rather than a divine order *of* history. By unfolding the Trinity into three historical ages (the age of the Father, of the Son, and—after 1260 according to Joachim's prophecy—the age of the Holy Spirit), Joachim of Fiore introduced the idea that God realizes His plan *in and through* history. For early Christians, no historical event reveals the *mystery* of God's economy of salvation. After Joachim of Fiore's claim that history does reveal God's plan after all, prophets return to the realm of possibility. But these new prophets must remain unarmed because it is *history itself* that will bring salvation "behind the backs" of political actors. This was Savonarola's idea of providence. The unarmed prophet is merely an interpreter of history, not a maker of history; he or she cannot accelerate the coming of the Messiah.

Looking now at the alternative Jewish conception of divine providence, we see that God enters human history as a military leader of his Chosen People, leading them in their wars to regain their "promised land"– which is a land on earth and not in a supernatural beyond—from other nations.[64] God's people is organized as an army, whose leader (Moses) follows the commands of God. The figure of the armed prophet (Moses) and the figure of the army commander are not different in early Jewish political theology. This explains why there is no confusion in Machiavelli when, later on in Chapter 26, he returns to his favorite theme of reorganizing a popular militia as the source of the new prince's *virtù* and the providential, redemptive mission to liberate and unify Italy. Indeed, all discourses on divine providence—including that of early Christians—rely on the analogy between God as the governor of the world and the commander of an army. This analogy originally derives from the image by which Aristotle's (and neo-Aristotelian) theology illustrates the proper relation between God and the world. It turns out that divine providence, understood in a theological-political fashion, is a discourse containing a theory of how people ought to go to war.

On a Catholic understanding of divine providence, the "military" order of the Catholic Church, composed of priests who love first God and then the world, is a military formation of believers dedicated to preserving the mystery of the economy of divine providence. The Church's conception of itself as an "army" of saints fighting sin is threatened by, and thus always opposes, the organization of a this-worldly people's army. But this is not the case in the Jewish conception of providence. Here the ordering of a republican people's army does not go against the logic of divine providence because within Hebrew political theology God's chosen commander of the people's army (Moses and later Joshua) is not an absolute sovereign, an absolute king. Rather, the basic postulate of Hebrew political theology is that Moses is the antithesis of a sovereign king. The Kingdom established through the Covenant of God with His people belongs to God, not to Moses. The "armed prophet" is there to ensure that no human king will rule God's people.

Read in light of this Hebrew political theology, Chapter 26 furnishes one of the first attempts to synthesize the model of the Hebrew Republic with the model of the Roman Republic; it is an experiment in political thinking that would prove absolutely decisive for the development of modern democratic political thought. The outcome of this experiment is that God's command over his people/army (namely, the regime that Josephus first called a "theocracy") is only realizable in the form of a democracy, that is, of a republic in which no human king commands the people. This conjunction of theocracy and democracy in the Hebrew Republic, prior to the period of the kings, is of absolute importance in Spinoza's argument that democracy is both the regime closest to natural right and God's favored form of government (whereby God is understood as Nature). Savonarola himself already spoke of "this government of the people being more natural."[65] Here we seem to have hit on a path that can reconcile providentialism with naturalism under a conception of politics that assigns priority to a people over a king or an aristocracy.

But one never steps in the same river twice, and a lot of water has passed since Chapter 6 where Machiavelli explicitly claims the new prince should not model himself on Moses because Moses had no free or armed people desirous of their freedom, which is the fundamental situation of all new princes. To be the commander of such a free and armed people, that is, what is at stake in Chapter 26, the new prince needs to model him or herself on another crucial figure of Hebrew political theology who is, in a sense, the counterpart of Moses: the Messiah.

The new prince must be a messianic captain of his or her people, because the Messiah, on the Jewish conception, is the last king of a people which is free and self-organized into an army. The Messiah is that paradoxical figure who "heads" a political body which desires not to be dominated and, for this reason, is willing to "cut the head off" any king (or Pope) who pretends to represent God on earth. We now know that, when kings' heads actually started rolling in Europe, once Machiavelli's thought was received in revolutionary England, the arguments revolutionaries employed against the idea of a kingship by "divine right" consisted in both the rediscovery of the Roman republican tradition (found in the *Discourses on Livy*) and in this new political reading of the relationship between Moses and the Messiah that resurfaces in *The Prince*.

The messianic expectation concerns the possibility of making a radical break with the past (which had been characterized by kingdoms and empires, rather than democracies) and opening a new future. In Florentine political thought in Machiavelli's time, this messianic possibility is referred to as the possibility of making a "return to beginnings," a return to the "first nature" of human beings. This formula of a "return to beginnings" is the deepest content of the Renaissance, and it is a formula that one finds both in Savonarola and in Ficino, as well as in Machiavelli: in all three it reflects the need to reform both religion and politics. But only in Machiavelli does the beginning to which all political order must periodically return refer to a radical equality of all with all, a return to a "state of nature" where human beings are considered to stand "naked," shorn of the acquired habits of inequality made possible by the division between rich and poor. Only in Machiavelli, just as in some conceptions of Jewish messianism, can the Messiah return an infinite amount of times, and therefore the messianic belief is compatible with the belief in the eternity of this world.

Likewise, the Jewish conception of providence, in contrast to the Christian idea of providence, does not preclude human beings from acting in ways that "force" or "accelerate" the arrival of the Messiah. There are certain special times when it is appropriate to "pray" for the arrival of the Messiah. Machiavelli's *Exhortation* in Chapter 26 seems to be just this kind of "prayer," which is said at the "right time." In one of his sermons, Savonarola refers to and chastises a saying by Cosimo de' Medici according to which "one does not govern a state by praying nor by reciting 'Our Father who art in Heaven'." Throughout *The Prince* Machiavelli seems to agree with Cosimo's saying. But now, at the end of the book, he addresses himself to a member of the Medici family in order to ironically subvert Cosimo's saying: sometimes politics needs to be messianic. But Machiavelli's messianism is not Savonarola's messianism. Machiavelli's prayer will be fulfilled only on condition that the time is right, and the criterion of rightness is whether the new prince has enough *virtù* to arm his or her own people. Not only is God unwilling to do everything and therefore awaits the right time to send the Messiah, Machiavelli is saying to the new Medici prince that only by becoming commander of an armed and free people will he have made himself in the image of God (as commander of His people) and be deserving of God's favor. Machiavelli ends his book as he started it: unless the Medici are willing to purify themselves of their sins, of their previous associations with the nobility and the kings of this world, and embrace the side of the people, then they will not live up to the image of God, and as a consequence God will not grace them with the salvation of their state.

STUDY QUESTIONS

1 Is Machiavelli's view of history a pessimistic or an optimistic one?
2 Does Machiavelli's theory of chance undermine or support his argument for self-reliance?
3 Is the belief that God intervenes in history an important question for politics?

CHAPTER NINE

Reception and influence

No other work in modern political thought, with the possible exception of Marx's *Communist Manifesto*, remotely competes with the influence exerted by Machiavelli's *Prince*. Thick tomes have been written on the history of its reception. This chapter will not recapitulate this complex history.[66] Rather, it discusses four main ways the work has been received in the last five hundred years, each of which bases its interpretation primarily on one of four themes highlighted in this *Reader's Guide*: evil, liberty, social conflict, and security. Thus, one of the earliest traditions of reception reacted to Machiavelli's advocacy of evil means in politics—already in Shakespeare's time, this gave rise to Machiavelli's satanic reputation as "murdrous Machiavel" (*Henry VI, Part III*); late into the twentieth century his name was still associated with totalitarian mass regimes and with covert actions undertaken by democratic governments such as Nixon's Watergate scandal or Kissinger's secret bombing of Cambodia. Second, the treatise was interpreted as a rhetorical and satirical exercise intended to demonstrate the illegitimate nature of principalities; on this interpretation, *The Prince* is a handbook for republican revolutionaries, exposing the workings of their enemy. Spinoza, Harrington, and Rousseau among others seem to have read *The Prince* in this way. The "republican" reading of Machiavelli was recovered in the last decades of the twentieth century, and Machiavelli identified as the founder of a modern conception of political freedom different from the liberal conception of negative liberty. Third, beginning in the early nineteenth century, with Fichte and Hegel, *The Prince* became

an inspiration for advocates of struggles of national independence
and the building of modern nation-states out of feudal social conditions. After the Russian Revolution, the treatise received a great
deal of attention from twentieth-century Marxist–Leninist thought,
especially once the Italian Marxist Antonio Gramsci identified
the role of the Communist party with that of Machiavelli's civil
prince. Fourth, the treatise was interpreted as the first example of
"reason of state;" as the first contribution to a modern conception
of government centered on the self-assertion of the state over all
particular social interests in the name of security. Since 9/11, many
analysts claim we have entered into a new age of security that has
given renewed valence to categories, such as the state of exception,
considered fundamental in the doctrine of reason of state. In what
follows we shall review what is at stake in these four traditions of
reception of *The Prince*.

Machiavelli, teacher of evil

There is no question that *The Prince* teaches the use of evil means
in the pursuit of legitimate political ends. But Machiavelli made
two additional points in relation to his way of introducing evil
into politics that were frequently forgotten by his subsequent critics
and admirers. The first one is that there is no novelty in the use
of evil means to the end of establishing good government. In *The
Prince* (Chapters 6 and 18) he suggests that anyone who reads the
Old Testament or "the ancient writers" (by which he means Greek
political thinkers like Plato) without prejudices will see that evil
means are advocated in both, though perhaps not as openly as he
dared. He also claims that his originality is not in having uncovered
the violent side of politics, but in trying to limit the use of evil
means to the function of providing freedom and security to those
who are subject to government.

   From rather early on, the accusation that Machiavelli's teaching
was evil or immoral came from that quarter which had an
interest in claiming that all political government ought to make
people "better" rather than leave them as they are (the latter
being Machiavelli's starting point): thus it became common for
the Christian faiths at war with each other in the sixteenth and

seventeenth centuries to accuse their enemies of "Machiavellian" practices. Throughout ancient and medieval political thought, it was taken for granted that government should lead people toward the "good life" or toward salvation. The good life was the life lived in imitation of the divine, hence it needed to be taught by those most familiar with the ways of divinity: the prophets who revealed divine laws and the priests who guided their application. On this standard, anyone who denied that a state ought to be modeled on a church, or who rejected the superiority of priestly government, or who recognized no divine laws over and above human laws, counts as a "teacher of evil."

Machiavelli's *Prince* is one of the first modern political works to propose a non-religious end to political activity; to argue not that the good life or eternal salvation, but freedom and security in this world, ought to be the ends pursued by political government. If, as the Christian religion teaches, to be a "good" person means to love God above the love of this world, then Machiavelli clearly did not adhere to this ranking of love objects. Rather, he reversed the ranking, and seems to have had a use only for that idea of divinity that was compatible with the love of the world. His complex attitude toward the use of religion for politics, his search for an idea of divinity that saw in a good light the human project of emancipation and enlightenment from authority and tradition, was one of the most influential legacies of Machiavelli's reception found in the deism of the English, American, and French revolutionaries. In this sense, Machiavelli was not irreligious, but rather one of the first to advocate the need for a modern civil religion based on the priority of people's freedom and security over and above their religious duties to the other-worldly Kingdom of God.

One of the most recent and influential attempts made to save Machiavelli from the accusation of being a teacher of evil was proposed by Isaiah Berlin. He argued that Machiavelli was not an immoralist, but rather adhered to a non-Christian morality, namely, that of pagan antiquity.[67] For Berlin, Machiavelli was perhaps the first liberal political philosopher because he had the audacity to question the belief in only one true model of a good life (just like there exists only one true God) and instead allowed for a plurality of conceptions of the good. Machiavelli is a relativist about ends (he acknowledges that equally valuable ends, such as freedom and justice, may not be equally realized by any given political system), but he is not immoral (if by this we mean that any means are justified to attain a given end). Berlin's contemporary, Leo Strauss, the best known recent advocate of the thesis that Machiavelli was a teacher of evil, also understood Machiavelli as a relativist because he gave up on the idea of a natural moral order of things and made the good relative to the need of human beings for security and control over their circumstances. For Strauss, Machiavelli set off the first "wave" of modern moral relativism which culminated with Nietzsche's nihilism, and whose effects were the totalitarian ideologies of the first half of the twentieth century.

The liberal and the totalitarian interpretations exemplify the range of possible readings one can give the problem of evil in Machiavelli's *Prince*. But both readings are questionable. Against Berlin's thesis, one can say that the values of individual freedom and security defended by Machiavelli are not, as such, values of pagan antiquity. Against Strauss's thesis, one can say that Machiavelli did hold on to an absolute source of value, namely, the belief that the world of becoming is eternal and offers a standard against which to measure all projects to improve humanity in a moral sense.

Machiavelli introduces evil into politics as a necessity designed to cope with the fact that most human beings "are not good" (Chapter 15). Many interpreters have located in this "anthropological pessimism" the key to Machiavelli's thinking about the problem of evil. Like other political thinkers, from Augustine through Hobbes to Schmitt, Machiavelli is said to hold the view that human beings are by nature "sinful" beings, in the sense that they are naturally aggressive and seek out enmity. Human beings will always divide themselves into groups of friends and enemies, and as a consequence war is both unavoidable in politics and should be the first and last concern of any political leadership. Given the aggressive nature of human beings, the best that one can aim at is to establish clear rules with regard to who has the right to go to war and who does not, and under what conditions.

As we saw, Machiavelli argues in *The Prince* that a state ought to rely on its armed subjects for its defense rather than on mercenary troops (Chapter 13), and that a statesman ought to focus primarily on matters of war and peace (Chapter 14). Both theses were very influential in the following centuries. Advocates of absolute rule, like Bodin and Hobbes, believed that war and violence (especially of a kind motivated by religion) could be contained only if one established a single, irresistible earthly judge or sovereign with the sole right to declare war and peace, to determine who are the friends and who are the enemies of the state. Opponents of absolute rule, instead, believed that war could be minimized, perhaps in the end eradicated, by instituting popular standing armies and by giving the people who were sent to war by their kings the right to decide whether to engage in war with other peoples or not. This belief was most radically represented by Kant's postulate that republics do not wage war against other republics. Not surprisingly, the discipline of international relations remains to date still characterized by a division between so-called realists, who plead the Hobbesian case for state sovereignty, and so-called idealists, who believe that Kant's postulate remains the only "scientific" law of political science.

Machiavelli, partisan of republicanism

Since Machiavelli was a faithful servant of the Florentine Republic, and in his later book *Discourses on Livy* went on to praise republics, many interpreters, amongst them Spinoza (in his *Political Treatise*) and Rousseau (*Social Contract*, book 3, Chapter 6), believe that he remained throughout his life a partisan of republican government. The conviction that Machiavelli had a political agenda, and was not simply an empirical political scientist happy to describe whatever regime he saw, gives rise to a second influential tradition according to which *The Prince* should not be read at face value, but as an ironical treatment of principalities designed to place modern republics in a good light. According to this line of interpretation, the "scientific" results obtained by Machiavelli in his treatise on principalities need to be relativized and comprehended within a larger context.

In recent decades, some interpreters have claimed the book was an occasional piece of writing that Machiavelli wrote while taking a break from his real intellectual project, his treatise on republics. Still others have argued that it reflected his political beliefs during his period in office, which would mature into an entirely different republican political theory once he went into exile.[68] If this is the case, why did Machiavelli go off on the tangent that is *The Prince*?

The reasons vary, from those who claim it was written purely for the practical reason of getting a job from the Medici, to those who identify in *The Prince* an answer to the crisis of republicanism in his times, when it seemed that absolute monarchies (the forerunners of modern nation-states), and not independent city states, were the political form of the future.[69] Other interpreters claim that *The Prince* was Machiavelli's contribution to an established genre and, more importantly, to an established way of thinking about state-craft (the "*arte dello stato*"); in this reading his theses on the state were occasionally original, but *The Prince* certainly does not count as a new start for modern political philosophy.[70] In the same vein, the *Discourses on Livy* are seen as Machiavelli's contribution to the other fundamental way of speaking about politics in his historical epoch, namely, the civic humanist language of "political" regimes synonymous with Aristotelian and Ciceronian rule of law and constitutional government.

The claim that Machiavelli exhibits a "dualistic" vision of politics in his two main works makes sense against the backdrop of the more general historical claim that in Italy, since the late medieval period, there was a continuous struggle between independent city states (republics) and principalities with each deriving their legitimation from very different discourses and sets of reasons. In this sense, the dualist interpretation claims that Machiavelli simply reflected and revised the legitimating discourses of both types of state, without thereby trying to formulate a third perspective on principalities and republics that understands their underlying unity.

The dualist thesis, which is shared by Baron and Skinner despite the fact that they disagree on the underlying causes of the opposition between republic and principality, has lately been questioned by scholars who reject the very idea of "civic humanism" as a doctrine friendly to republics and an enemy of principalities. These interpreters argue that civic humanists like Bracciolini and Bruni are not republican partisans but, first and foremost, teachers of rhetoric who praise, both in republics and in principalities, the fact of prudent, élite rule which is itself modeled on the classical political philosophy of Plato and Aristotle.[71] Some interpreters like Bausi deny entirely the claim that Machiavelli was ever a partisan of republicanism, believing instead that, after the downfall of the Florentine Republic, Machiavelli wrote *The*

Prince to convince defenders of republican self-government that the way forward led toward the new absolute monarchies of France, Spain, and England. On this view, Machiavelli denies the difference between principality and republic in favor of the former.

Despite these objections, the general consensus is that the combined historical work of Baron, Pocock, and especially Skinner has managed to establish the fact that Machiavelli's thought condensed an understanding of republican liberty that became fundamental for the anti-monarchic Atlantic Revolutions, from the English revolution to the American, French, and Haitian revolutions, followed by the establishment of the republics of Latin America. What remains an object of polemic is the content of this republican idea of liberty. What is its provenance? When does it emerge in the late medieval or early Renaissance period? Is it essentially different from the later, liberal interpretation of modern liberty?

The starting point of the discussion is the idea of "civic humanism" or "classical republicanism" brought to light by the work of Baron and Gilbert in the late 1930s and early 1940s. At first, it was thought that this ideology of the independent city-state owed its origin indistinctly to the reception of Aristotle and Cicero. As the historiography of the concept of liberty progressed, the distinction between a neo-Aristotelian republicanism and a neo-Roman or Ciceronian republicanism widened into two incompatible visions of freedom. The former has been defended by Pocock, while the latter has been taken up by Skinner and Pettit.[72] Pocock argued for the decisive importance of the reception of Aristotle's *Politics* in early Renaissance thought, and in particular of the figure of the citizen-soldier. At issue here was the ideal of positive freedom, namely, the Aristotelian claim that a good life can only be achieved if the human being becomes a full-time political actor and completely projects his or her life onto the political life of his or her city or nation. To be free meant to give priority to one's duties toward the community over one's individual rights or immunities against the political community.

For Skinner and Pettit, on the other hand, republicanism preceded the re-discovery of Aristotle's *Politics* in the West because it is tied to the resurgence of a "neo-Roman" idea of liberty, tied to the recovery of Cicero and rhetoric in the independent Italian city-states of the late Middle Ages. Here freedom is understood as a negative, not a positive, form of liberty. In other words, one is free not in virtue of participation in self-government, but in virtue of enjoying the absence of some constraint. According to Skinner and Pettit, the neo-Roman ideal of liberty means that one is free as long as one is not dominated, and that means as long as no one has a master. But to have no masters is just to be ruled by the coercion of laws made by the entire commonwealth rather than by the arbitrary will and decisions of some individuals. The status of being a freeman cannot be secured except when power is constitutionally distributed among all citizens and does not reside in the hands of an absolute sovereign. For Skinner, the English revolutionaries were motivated more by this neo-Roman idea of freedom than by a neo-Aristotelian idea of civic virtue when they executed their king.

Since the debate between Pocock and Skinner on the origins and nature of republican liberty, a third narrative about Atlantic republicanism has emerged in the wake of Strauss's interpretation of Machiavelli, which highlights the "modernity" of the Florentine thinker. On this interpretation, Machiavelli's republicanism is "modern" because it makes a clean break with both neo-Aristotelian and neo-Ciceronian forms of civic humanism. Machiavelli is said to reject the humanist reception of Aristotle because he splits the goal of political action from the achievement of the good or happy life, and as a consequence political virtue is no longer identical to the virtue of justice. He also rejects the humanist reception of Cicero because he divorces the legitimacy of republican coercive law from natural law, thus opening up the modern possibility of a republicanism without natural law. For these interpreters, when Machiavelli rejected natural law he rejected the claim that wisdom (whether granted by philosophy or by divine revelation) is the highest title to rule over the many. Following Strauss, they claim that such a denial of wisdom was made possible by the "Epicurean" basis of modern freedom already found in Machiavelli, which gives priority to the satisfaction of individual interests (essentially by securing the right to private property above all other rights), and fosters an aggressive and imperialistic politics on the part of the new so-called republics in view of satisfying the desires of the masses.[73] In other words, against both Pocock and Skinner, these interpreters bring Machiavelli's republicanism much closer to later versions of liberalism.

Both sides of this on-going debate make valid points. Pocock and Skinner are right when they uncover a republican, not liberal, ideal of modern liberty in the work of Machiavelli. On the other hand, they tend to downplay the sense in which Machiavelli's republicanism is "modern" and breaks with both the Aristotelian and Ciceronian traditions. But this is not to say that all modern political thought is necessarily "liberal," as the neo-Straussian narrative has it. Rather, when Spinoza and Rousseau praised *The Prince* for being a covert handbook for republican revolutionaries they saw the potential contained in discarding natural law (or the wisdom of the few) as the ground of legitimacy of the state because it opened the path for a democratic form of legitimation, where coercive law is legitimate only when an entire people judges that it could have given this law to itself. For Rousseau, what is right cannot be derived from any "natural law" because right can only refer to those conditions of an original social contract (hence, from an agreement between free and equal individuals) which establishes a sovereign people—conditions which correspond to the untrammeled, because rational, exercise of the "free will" of human beings and not to its subjection to a natural, rational order. One of the key links from Machiavelli's rejection of natural law to Rousseau's new republican understanding of legitimacy is Spinoza, the most important early modern philosopher to have admired *The Prince*. Spinoza's conception of right or legitimacy also explicitly breaks with "natural law" theories while simultaneously offering the ground for one of the first defenses of popular sovereignty. For Spinoza, "the natural right of every man is determined not by sound reason, but by his desire and his power."[74] It follows that the more power one has, the more right one has; therefore a democracy (or republic) that unites the power of all individuals (i.e., which is based on the power of the people) will have the greatest right or legitimacy of all forms of government. Spinoza and Rousseau offer strong evidence that a republicanism without natural law need not be identical to modern liberalism, as the Straussian interpretation has it.

Machiavelli, communist *avant la lettre*

All of the above neo-republican interpretations of Machiavelli tend to underplay the advocacy of violence and the primordial dimension of class or social conflict between people and élites that Machiavelli brought to light in *The Prince*. Yet one cannot think about modern republican revolutions without considering the extreme violence through which they are born: many eggs are broken for the sake of establishing a new order of individual freedom and security. Modern republican revolutions are also social movements that overcome the dualism between people and élite, as modern popular revolutions are always initiated by an (intellectual) élite. These two facts about modern revolutions lend credence to a third kind of reception of Machiavelli's *Prince*, one which follows the guiding thread of social struggle, as opposed to those of evil and of liberty. This reception discards the "dualist" picture of Machiavelli and seeks a standpoint from which both *The Prince* and the *Discourses on Livy* appear as two sides of one and the same unitary, revolutionary political project. Indeed, although Spinoza and Rousseau may have advocated the "republican" reading of *The Prince*, they did not stop there; they were seeking to establish a republican *state*, a popular form of *sovereignty*, and thus were just as interested in what Machiavelli had to say about the *stato* and about the prerogatives of the new prince (sovereignty), as in what he said about republics and the rule of law.

While the neo-republican interpretation of Machiavelli gives a lot of importance to the role played by legal coercion in the securing of a state of non-domination, it forgets that for Machiavelli laws are but one way of fighting war, the other being force (Chapter 18). Thus, for Machiavelli, coercive laws are the pointers of an on-going social conflict. Any regime that rules by laws, on this picture, has managed to erase the traces of on-going social conflict and transformed such conflict into social peace, or, in more contemporary parlance, such a regime has attained hegemony. This understanding of law as the means by which violence legitimates itself is opposed to Hobbes's modern natural right doctrine because it denies the existence of a clear break, at some point in the historical past, between the state of nature and the civil condition, legitimating once and for all the current holders of supreme power. The alternative view is based on the positive revaluation of social and political conflicts as events in the history of a commonwealth through which the hegemony of a class or élite is questioned and possibly reversed, helping transform legal domination into a true rule of law where no one is dominated. The internal relation between law, violence, ideology, and social conflict that Machiavelli placed at the heart of *The Prince* (Chapters 7 through 9) became very influential with the strand of radical republican thinking represented by radical French Huguenots like Hotman and radical democrats like the Levellers in England, which denied that absolute monarchies had successfully imposed peace. This radical republicanism later fed into what became known as the socialist and communist movements and their way of understanding revolutionary politics.

Revolutions are fleeting events and history teaches that, unless they give rise to strong state constitutions, their gains may be lost. How to build a lasting state from the anarchic moment of revolutionary freedom became a serious concern after the Atlantic revolutions, and what many thinkers inclined to socialism and communism saw as their limitations: after all, the American revolution maintained the institution of slavery and it took another civil war to abolish it; the French revolution gave way to Napoleon; the Haitian revolution left hardly any traces and was followed by centuries of colonialism and imperialism; the republics of Latin America were quickly taken over by a never-ending succession of dictatorships and authoritarian regimes, up to our own days. The idea that real freedom and equality, in the end, can be established not by a self-governed people, not in a direct-democratic way, but by a state (or prince) that represents the people's desire for freedom (their general will), was something that Fichte and Hegel appreciated in Machiavelli's *Prince*. They understood *The Prince* as teaching that a free people and a strong constitutional and representative state must come about at the same time. To be a free people is the same as to will a strong state of their own. Hence for both Fichte and Hegel the republican *Discourses on Livy* could not be divorced from *The Prince* because a true republican state constitution could only arise out of a "constituent power" that necessarily operated from a situation of a-legality, from a degree zero of legitimacy, just as Machiavelli had described the actions and intentions of the new prince.

In general, the reception of Machiavelli in the Marxist tradition follows and radicalizes the above interpretation, so that *The Prince* is understood to exemplify the kinds of actions needed to achieve a revolution, whilst the *Discourses on Livy* describes the kinds of actions needed to establish hegemony and build a free state that lasts in time. Thus, Lenin will argue that a communist revolution requires the violent conquest of the bourgeois state and the establishment of a dictatorship of the proletariat as a means to attain a communist society. Although in the communist ideal there should be no place for the sovereignty of the state, still Lenin argued against the advocates of spontaneous popular revolt like Rosa Luxemburg that, without the conquest of the state at the hands of the new worker's élite organized around a Communist party, no revolution would ever succeed. Just as Machiavelli suggested that the violence of the new prince could extinguish all traces of the legitimacy of hereditary monarchy, so Lenin believed that the dictatorship of the proletariat could wipe away the legitimacy of bourgeois constitutional government.

The inability to reproduce a communist revolution in Western liberal democracies led the Italian Marxist Gramsci to offer a new reading of *The Prince*, according to which the rule of the bourgeoisie over society was not simply dependent on their control of the state and their monopoly of violence, but also on their hegemony over society exerted by non-violent means like law and education. Gramsci suggested that the state would be conquered only once the Communist party wrested this hegemony from the hands of the bourgeoisie. This struggle was not decided by arms, by pitting one class against the rest of society, but it consisted in the Communist party coming to play the role of a new "civil prince" who was capable of coalescing around itself a new "people," by forming new alliances with other disenfranchised parts of society, and thus leaving to the élites of the bourgeoisie the role of the "foreign" invader that needed to be expelled from power, possibly even by peaceful means like democratic elections.[75]

Starting in the late 1960s, with the student, feminist, gay, and anti-colonial struggles for liberation, it became quickly evident that no Communist party could build a successful coalition and still maintain the priority assigned to the industrial proletariat class by Marxist theory. Once again, it was through another interpretation of the relation between *The Prince* and the *Discourses on Livy* that post-Marxist thought articulated itself, essentially in the work of Lefort, Althusser, and Laclau. All three recognize in the "civil prince" not so much the heroic representative of the revolutionary classes, but a flawed, partial representative of the fact of social struggle. Thus, Lefort argues that the conflict between those who wish to rule over others and those who wish not to be dominated, in any society, can never be resolved by any state. Since the unity of a people can never be represented politically, the best that can be done is to defend the rights of anyone who wishes to see their interests represented by the state; this in turn requires strengthening the rule of law against the claims made by state sovereignty.

Althusser, for his part, claims that Machiavelli correctly identified the distinction between the perspective of the "civil prince" or state and the perspective of the "people" based on the fact of social conflict, but he could not offer a way to bridge this distance between them. Althusser understands Machiavelli's republicanism as an admission that the legal power of the state, along with its other ideological instruments, can always cover up the existence of a real class or social conflict, transforming the revolutionary claims of people into reformist electoral platforms. The *Discourses on Livy* with its emphasis on the rule of law takes over *The Prince* with its revolutionary, state-creating prince: for Althusser, the constituent power of the "civil prince" is always a function of the legitimacy of the constituted power of law. It is as if the Constitution of the United States retroactively invents for itself the myth of the Revolution, knowing all too well that there will be no further revolution that can break the Constitution and really begin anew.

Lastly, Laclau has perhaps most influentially shown that there is no "fact" of social or class struggle at all, as the state belongs to whichever "civil prince" is capable of fashioning alliances between social groups that understand themselves as the "people" fighting against some common "enemy." According to Laclau, this fight can be picked around whatever issue is most convenient for forming the winning coalition, but having nothing to do with a primordial social division or conflict, such as that between the rich and the poor. The conflict around whether gay couples should have the right to marry might serve to coalesce a new hegemony just as much, if not more than, any conflict around wealth distribution. With Laclau, Machiavelli's *Prince* ceases to be the prophecy of Marxist class struggle and becomes the advice book of all "populist" leaders, irrespective of their party adherence.[76]

Machiavelli, inventor of "reason of state"

Of all the traditions of interpretation of Machiavelli's *Prince*, perhaps the most influential one remains that of "reason of state."[77] This term refers to the sum of actions and policies needed in order to acquire, preserve, and enlarge the power of the state in the name of providing security. Although Machiavelli did not employ the term himself (it was first coined by Giovanni Botero, an Italian Catholic priest, in 1589), the fundamental belief of reason of state, that government is a sphere with rules of its own that are not reducible to moral principles, is clearly traceable to the influence of *The Prince*. These rules concern what must be done when a state of necessity or exception puts at risk the safety of the state, and along with it the security of its population. After Machiavelli's death and the success of the Reformation, a period of religious wars overwhelmed most countries of Europe. It appeared likely that government policy could be dominated by religious, sectarian interests, leading to protracted and international civil wars. Reason of state doctrine emerges in this context as a way to prop up the interests of the subjects in having a strong and functioning state that permits the orderly development of their worldly interests rather than assuring their other-worldly salvation. Reason of state gives a positive content to Machiavelli's "teaching of evil" and in that way makes it acceptable.

Throughout *The Prince* Machiavelli labored to distinguish the government of priests from government based on the state. Priestly government justifies itself by appeal to the religious and moral doctrines it tries to advance; state-based government, on the other hand, takes as its supreme goal the security and liberty of its subjects. At times, particularly when political conditions veer toward civil war, statesmen may have to engage in actions that would not be condoned if performed by civilians in order to maintain the integrity of the state. Reason of state adopts Machiavelli's concepts of necessity and of a proper use of cruelty as the hallmarks of state action.

Necessity and violence come together in a central idea of the doctrine of reason of state, namely, the idea of a *coup d'État*, first theorized by Gabriel Naudé (1639). By *coup d'État* is meant a violent action undertaken by the state that shakes up society and allows the state to regain the upper hand in the conduct of government; it is an action through which the state re-establishes its own "health" or condition, which may have been undermined or threatened by its being called to serve contradictory, social, and particular interests, rather than the interest of state.

Because the object of government is the security and liberty of its population, reason of state doctrine widened the spectrum for the intervention of the state; from running the economy to establishing a state religion, all activities become legitimate concerns of government. From the perspective of reason of state, everything in society is potentially a "political" issue as long as it threatens the security and liberty of some of the subjects of the state. Following Machiavelli's intuition that politics emerges from war, and pursuing its general maxim that anything can be political, reason of state doctrine sets itself the major task of governing the conduct of war between states. After bringing to an end the period of religious wars, adherents of reason of state attempted to establish the bases of a new world political order, sometimes referred to as the system resulting from the Treaty of Westphalia. The basis of this world order is the idea of maintaining an equilibrium of forces between national states. This doctrine of a balance of power allows states to make "good use" of cruelty by engaging in war as a continuation of diplomacy (Clausewitz).

With regard to internal politics, the maxim that anything social can be a matter for government control gives rise to a science of police (*Polizeiwissenschaft*), to be distinguished from the science of politics (having to do with the design of state institutions), and which today we refer to by the term "public policy." According to one of its earliest exponents, Johann H. G. von Justi, the function of the police is neither to acquire the state nor to conserve it, but rather to increase its power by providing for the welfare of its population. Reason of state becomes increasingly a matter of population statistics: making sure that the numbers of the population increase by providing for the necessities of life, the health of the inhabitants, their productive occupation, and, lastly, for the safety in the circulation and commerce of and between things and persons.

But it is precisely the rise of commercial society, based on the free exchange of commodities and labor, and the rise of civil society, based on the free exchange of opinions, that led to the crisis of reason of state in the eighteenth and nineteenth centuries. The new science of political economy discovered that not only the state, but also society, has rules of its own. These rules turned out to be, partially at least, beyond the reach of state manipulation and intervention. The security and liberty of subjects was increasingly understood in terms of a system of needs (the free market) and a system of rights (the legal order) which limits from the outside the interference of legitimate state government. These conditions gave rise to the doctrine of liberalism, the idea that the best results for the population are achieved not by making everything "political" but by limiting the reach of government intervention and adopting a policy of *laissez-faire* with respect to the circulation of commodities as well as of opinions. For liberalism, a good government is one that acknowledges the limits imposed by law and economics on the state. In this sense, one can say that the advent of liberalism spells the end of the hegemony of reason of state. For this reason, it is not uncommon to find interpreters who tend to think that "liberalism" and "Machiavellism" are antonyms. The relatively recent formulation of a liberal theory of justice in the work of Rawls has brought back a Kantian form of political moralism, which, under the name of "public reason," seeks to establish itself as the alternative standard for public conduct to that represented by the tradition of "reason of state."

Since Machiavelli wrote *The Prince* five hundred years ago, these four distinct receptions have known alternating fortunes, but none of them has ever disappeared; on the contrary they seem to return eternally. During the twentieth century, triggered by world economic crises and as a reactionary response to the advent of the Russian Revolution, totalitarian mass regimes emerged in Italy, Germany, and Spain. Mussolini, Hitler, and Franco imagined themselves to be the "new princes" charged with militarizing their societies and extending absolute control of the state on every feature of human life. They brought back the "murderous Machiavel" in their fight against both liberal and socialist ideals. At the end of World War Two a new design for the state, called the welfare state, was charged to bring together the best of liberalism with the best of socialism. But this experiment in statecraft was unable to navigate the contrary demands of socialism for a planned economy and of neo-liberalism for a minimal government, and as a consequence the welfare state model succumbed in the last decades of the twentieth century. Since then, the neo-republican interpretation of Machiavelli has re-emerged with renewed vigor as an alternative between an absolute and a minimal conception of government. But a true republican model of state capable of coping with the challenges of a globalized economy and civil society is still not available, and in the new age of security a republican theory of public reason still needs to cope with the problems highlighted by reason of state, namely, the tension between security and liberty. How to piece together Machiavelli "the author of the *Prince* and republican citizen"[78] remains a challenge not only for scholars but also for the future of democratic politics.

But whether it is in order to manipulate and terrorize them, to organize them and lead them to freedom, or to manage their security and pursuit of happiness, all four traditions of interpretation share a common feature: they understand that the revolutionary achievement of *The Prince* was to place the people's desires as the fundamental material which governments and statesmen have at their disposal and on which they need to work. It is on the adulation, judgment or opinion of their people that states and statesmen ultimately rely. Having brought to light this rebellious material, and the limits with which it confronts the resources of political philosophy, is the signal theoretical achievement of *The Prince*.

NOTES

1 "The most elevated political thought and the most varied forms of human development are found united in the history of Florence, which in this sense deserves the name of the first modern state in the world. Here the whole people are busied with what in the despotic cities is the affair of a single family" (Burckhardt, 1958, 95).

2 For general accounts of Machiavelli's life and works, I have consulted Viroli (1998), Bausi (2005), and Inglese (2006). On Machiavelli's early political career, I have benefited from Black (2010), Pesman (2010), and Butters (2010).

3 One of the best accounts of Savonarola's appeal remains George Eliot's period novel, *Romola*.

4 "He, if anybody, could have secularized the States of the Church, and he would have been forced to do so in order to keep them. Unless we are much deceived, this is the real reason of the secret sympathy with which Machiavelli treats the great criminal; from Cesare or from nobody, could it be hoped that he 'would draw the steel from the wound'; in other words, annihilate the Papacy – the source of all foreign intervention and of all the divisions of Italy" (Burkhardt, 1958, 130).

5 See Gilbert (1949).

6 From a letter written by one of his followers, discussed in Bausi (2005), 89–90.

7 On the Medici, see Brown (1992).

8 Kantorowicz (1997) and Bayona Aznar (2007).

9 The following discussion on civic humanism relies on the classic studies of Baron (1988), Pocock (1975), Rubinstein (2004), Skinner (2002), Nederman (2009).

10 Bracciolini in Kraye (1997), 136.

11 On Poggio's discovery of Lucretius, see Greenblatt (2011).

12 Bruni in Griffiths (2000), 124.

13 See Gilbert (1939) and Stacey (2007).

14 See Brown (2010) on the reception of Lucretius in Renaissance Florence.

15 On astral theology and Renaissance esoteric religious motifs, see Ludueña Romandini (2006).

16 Cassirer (1974), Strauss (1958), Voegelin (1952).

17 For this historicist perspective on Machiavelli, see Baron (1988) and Pocock (1975).

18 Skinner (2002).

19 Najemy (2006) and Fubini (1992) on civic humanism as ideology.

20 For other presentations of Machiavelli as the architect of a democratic project of modernity, see Mansfield (1996) and McCormick (2011).

21 Figgis (1960) is perhaps the first to see Machiavelli's importance in his critique of natural law.

22 See Baron (1988), 101–51.

23 On Lucretius and Machiavelli, see Ruiz Stull (2009), Morfino (2006), Rahe (2007).

24 For various arguments supporting this claim, I refer to Vatter (2000), Rahe (2009), McCormick (2011), Lefort (2012), Althusser (2011).

25 For this argument, see Stacey (2007).

26 On the absence of "state" in medieval political life, see Grossi (2004).

27 I owe this point to Ménissier (2001).

28 On the sacral foundations of monarchies, see Oakley (2006).

29 Much ink has been spent on whether Machiavelli's reference to a work on republics means that he had already written a version of the *Discourses* before he began work on the *Prince* or if, on the contrary, he wrote the *Prince* before the *Discourses* but amended at a later stage his text and thus included a reference to his later work on republics. The latter version is now the standard hypothesis, but it is impossible to prove philologically the exact chronology of all the parts of the *Prince* and the *Discourses*.

30 This point is made by Figgis (1960) as well as by Ginzburg (2003), among others.

31 On classical accounts of the origin of political communities, see Syros (2011).

32 On civil religion, see Silk (2004).

33 A point first made by Strauss (1957).

34 For the primacy of social conflict in Machiavelli, see the arguments in Lefort (2012), Lucchese (2011), Geuna (2005).

35 I rely here on Larivaille (2001).

36 Marx (1975), 230.

37 On the "theatrical" display of Borgia, see Kahn (1994).

38 On the difference between liberal and republican ideals of liberty in relation to Machiavelli, compare Skinner (2002) and Pettit (1999) with Sullivan (2004).

39 On Machiavelli's views of the Church, see Cutinelli-Rendina (1998).

40 For a wide-ranging discussion on Machiavelli's hostility to the nobility, see McCormick (2011).

41 Cicero (1991), II, 41–2, p.78.

42 On Roman ideas of princes, see Stacey (2007).

43 For Machiavelli's critique of Cicero, see Skinner (1981); for his critique of Plato, see Strauss (2000).

44 Cicero (1991), II, 73, pp.92–3.

45 Cicero (1991), I, 15, p.7.

46 Cicero (1991), I, 23, p.10, and Cicero (1991), I, 42, p.19.

47 Cicero (1991), II, 43, p.79.

48 On this concept, see Pitkin (1967).

49 Cicero (1991), II, 23, p.71.

50 Cicero (1991), I, 34, p.14.

51 Cicero (1991), I, 41, pp.18–19.

52 Robert Musil (1930–42), *Man Without Qualities* [*Der Mann ohne Eigenschaften*]. 3 vols, Austria: Rowohlt.

53 On this possibility, see Strauss (2000).

54 Plato (1980), 709b-c.

55 Plato (1980), 710a.

56 Plato (1980), 710d.

57 Plato (1980), 708d.

58 Marsilio Ficino, Letter to Giovanni Rucellai, cited in Warburg (1996), 235.

59 Cited in Warburg (1996), 237. For image see link: http://www.britishmuseum.org/system_pages/beta_collection_introduction/

beta_collection_object_details.aspx?objectId=755357&partId=1&sea
rchText=rucellai

60 On the Lazy Argument, I rely on Vuillemin (1984).

61 On this point, see Santoro (1966).

62 This interpretation is most forcibly made by Sasso (1993).

63 The best discussion of divine providence in Machiavelli is found in
    Martelli (1982).

64 On this point, I follow the studies of Buber (1964).

65 Such a joining of theocracy with democracy is already prefigured
    by Savonarola (*Ruth e Micae*, 18 May 1496): "Your government,
    Florence, is similar to that of the Judges of the Israelites. ... This
    government of the Hebrews, although it was democratic [popolare],
    because the people governed and the judges did not rule, but merely
    offered counsels, could also be called a regal government [governo
    regale] because it depended on the mouth of one, namely, of God,
    because God told them what they had to do through the mouth of
    the judge and of the prophet" [translation mine].

66 Brief accounts of the reception of Machiavelli's work I consulted are
    Kahn (2010) and Cutinelli-Rendina (1999).

67 Berlin (1980).

68 Chabod (1958), Sasso (1993), and Baron (1988).

69 Bausi (2005).

70 Baron (1988), Skinner (2002), and Viroli (2005).

71 See the contributions in Hankins (2000).

72 For a clear discussion of this debate, see Geuna (2006).

73 Rahe (2009).

74 Spinoza (ch.16).

75 On Gramsci and Machiavelli, see Fontana (1983).

76 Laclau (2007).

77 For this discussion of reason of state, I rely on Meinecke (1998) and
    Foucault (2009).

78 Baron (1988).

NOTES FOR FURTHER READING

As often happens with authors who did not write their works in English, much of the best secondary literature on their work is also not to be found in English translation. In the case of Machiavelli, this literature is in Italian, with significant contributions found in French and Spanish. Since I have benefited from this scholarship in writing this *Reader's Guide*, it is only fair that I mention selected works from it below, along with selected works in English, for those readers interested in further study of the questions touched upon in the above chapters.

On Machiavelli's education and culture (Chapter One)

Italian scholarship on Machiavelli is particularly strong with regard to the study of his historical and cultural context, and on the question of his education and the extent of his knowledge of the classics. Probably the most important Machiavelli scholar of the twentieth century on these themes is Sasso (1987–8 and 1993). Unfortunately, none of his works are translated into English. Among his most significant contributions is the collection of essays, *Machiavelli e gli antichi e altri saggi*, in four volumes which touch on virtually every topic related to Machiavelli. Some of these essays are dedicated to one chapter of one book of Machiavelli, and they can each be as long as this *Reader's Guide*.

Perhaps due to their daunting erudition, Sasso's writings give the impression that Machiavelli was an omniscient intellectual who formulated every one of his hypotheses with full knowledge of Greek and Roman philosophy, literature, and historiography. Sasso defends the thesis that Machiavelli was a systematic thinker and that his varied production shares one and the same philosophical and political vision, which is essentially a tragic vision of human freedom fighting to secure a place for itself in a hostile world. This picture of Machiavelli's culture and of his writing has been seriously called into question in the work of Martelli (2009) and Bausi (2005). Both present Machiavelli as having had only a rough knowledge of the classics, often citing them by heart and mistakenly, and as more at ease with popular Florentine culture. Most importantly, these commentators see Machiavelli as a thinker who never wrote systematically but always as a response to contingent social and political events, and who changed his theses over time and according to opportunities. Bausi and Martelli deny that Machiavelli was a consistent republican, and place him politically much closer to the Medici regime and to its ideology than heretofore thought. More recently, Ginzburg (2003 and 2009) has contributed to the growing literature on Machiavelli's early education and on his creative reception of humanism, pointing out his important debt to scholasticism.

In English scholarship, Skinner (1978, 1981, 2002) has made a decisive contribution to our picture of Machiavelli, arguing forcibly for a contextual study of his works and showing the importance of rhetorical studies on Machiavelli's development and on the history of Renaissance political ideas in general. By way of contrast, Italian scholarship tends to emphasize either Machiavelli's philosophical formation (Sasso) or his literary (poetical) formation (Martelli and Bausi). Godman (1998) also shed new light on Machiavelli's complex relationship to Florentine humanists and for his apprenticeship in rhetoric.

On Machiavelli as political scientist, rhetorician, and philosopher (Chapter Two)

The status of Machiavelli's *Prince* has been a highly disputed question in recent scholarship: is it a work of political science, of rhetoric, or of philosophy? Among the many interpreters who see

The Prince as the first example of a modern empirical political science, one can still learn a great deal from Cassirer (1974) and Aron (1993). For Machiavelli's relationship to Leonardo da Vinci as an example of the attempt to apply natural science to politics, see the recent study by Masters (1999).

The importance of the tradition of rhetoric in order to understand Machiavelli's *Prince* finds convincing illustrations in Kahn (1994) and Skinner (2002), among others. Skinner pioneered an approach to the interpretation of texts according to which the most important question for understanding a text is to discern what the author was trying to do by writing the text and, more particularly, against what other texts or standpoints does the work stand in a polemical relation.

A very different approach is held by those interpreters who read Machiavelli as a philosopher intent on creating an entirely new vision of politics and breaking with his familiar contexts: thus Althusser (2011) speaks of Machiavelli's "solitude" with respect to his age, and Strauss (1958) shows Machiavelli as a philosopher grappling with the "eternal" problems of political philosophy bequeathed by Plato and Aristotle, giving them an opposite, yet equally philosophical answer. For a more recent and less partisan understanding of Machiavelli's work as systematic in a philosophical sense, see Ménissier (2010). Rahe (2000) is a useful exercise that attempts to situate the discussion between a rhetorical and a philosophical approach to Machiavelli.

On Machiavelli's intentions in writing *The Prince* (Chapter Three)

At least from Spinoza onward it was assumed, and with good reasons, that Machiavelli had a secret agenda in writing *The Prince*. Despite the fact that Machiavelli's book treats of princes and is dedicated to a prince, many have read the work as having another subject matter and other addressees in mind. The most imaginative and extreme esoteric reading of Machiavelli remains Strauss (1957). According to Strauss, Machiavelli pursues an ambitious theologico-political project of replacing the Bible as a fundamental ethical reference point in the West, going well beyond the nominal project of uniting Italy under the state of the new prince. This line of interpretation has been followed by Mansfield (1996) and Sullivan (1996), among others. An equally sophisticated esoteric reading of Machiavelli, written as a response to Strauss, can be found in Lefort (2012), who portrays Machiavelli as having the project of undermining class-based society and politics. McCormick (2011) is an example of how this line of interpretation still remains productive today. For a more traditional version of Machiavelli's intention of subverting the figure of the prince, see Stacey (2009), who remains within the rhetorical paradigm.

On Machiavelli's ideas of state and republic (Chapter Four)

For a long time it was assumed that Machiavelli's central innovation consisted in his idea of the state, which was said to anticipate the Weberian definition of the modern state as the legitimate exercise of domination over a determined territory thanks to the monopoly of violence. This was the view of Meinecke (1998) and Chabod (1958), which contain much on Machiavelli's notion of *stato* that is still valid. Mansfield (1996) remains within this Weberian picture of Machiavelli's state but emphasizes the importance of the direct relation between executive and people that leaves to the side both parliamentarism and constitutionalism.

Skinner (2002 and 2009) and Viroli (2005) have argued that in Machiavelli there subsists a dualism between a late medieval or neo-Roman conception of the republic and an early modern idea of the state; indeed, they suggest that Machiavelli addressed both ideas separately in the *Discourses on Livy* and *The Prince*, respectively. On this picture, there are two incompatible ways of thinking about the state that survive in modernity: one is republican, giving pride of place to the political self-organization of a people in parliamentarism and constitutionalism, and the other is absolutist, turning on the sovereignty of the state. But this dualistic picture makes it difficult to account for the fact that no modern republican thinker separates republic from state in the above manner (see Rousseau or Kant, or even Rawls).

On Machiavelli's ideas of social conflict and of civil principality (Chapter Five)

Some of the most exciting developments in Machiavellian studies during the last decade have been driven by taking seriously his discovery that every political organization of society is to be understood as a response to underlying and on-going social conflicts; in short, that social conflict is politically productive. Among the contributions to this way of reading *The Prince* see Vatter (2000), Gaille-Nikodimov (2004), del Lucchese (2011), and McCormick (2011). Najemy (2000) and Fubini (1992) provide good accounts of social conflict in Florence as the fundamental context within which to understand Machiavelli's theses.

Closely related to the problem of social conflict is Machiavelli's idea of the civil principality. The meaning of the term, and its importance to Machiavelli's overall discourse, remain highly contested. Some interpreters like Sasso (1987–8) see the civil prince as Machiavelli's positive political project in response to the failure of the Florentine Republic, whereas others like Baron and Larivaille (1982) believe Machiavelli's discussion of the civil prince shows the inherent weaknesses of all principalities in dealing with social conflict, thus signaling his intention to move toward republics as the better political form.

On Machiavelli's idea of war (Chapter Six)

Paradoxically, for someone who placed war and empire at the center of politics, the study of Machiavelli's ideas on war has not received as much attention in the secondary literature. Fournel and Zancarini (2003) have written an important history of the Italian wars during Machiavelli's times that provides the context within which he developed his fundamental idea of a popular militia as basis of the state. Hörnquist (2004) is the most complete study of the notion of empire in Machiavelli and in humanist thought. Barthas (2012) provides the most detailed and sophisticated account of Machiavelli's project of the militia and its relation to his incipient economic theory available to date.

On Machiavelli and the "mirror of princes" (Chapter Seven)

Machiavelli's debt toward and revision of the "mirror of princes" genre is one of the oldest topics in Machiavelli scholarship. The classic article by Gilbert (1939) still remains valid, in particular because it clearly identifies the fundamental role played by the rediscovery of Platonism, and of Hellenistic ideas of kingship in general, on the development of the humanist ideal of the prince and its influence on Machiavelli. Stephens (1988), Skinner (2002), and Stacey (2007) have, for their part, argued that the Roman accounts of principalities (especially in Cicero and Seneca) remain the decisive accounts Machiavelli wished to subvert in *The Prince*. One of the most interesting recent innovations in this line of inquiry comes from the comparative study of the "mirror of princes" genre as exemplified by Springborg (1992) and Syros (2012).

On Machiavelli, chance and divine providence (Chapter Eight)

The closing meditations on the role of chance and divine providence are fundamental if one wishes to understand better Machiavelli's basic philosophical standpoint. For the Renaissance discussion on chance and determinism Cassirer (1963) remains the best introduction; the latest and most complete discussion of the tension between freedom and determinism in Machiavelli is found in Saralegui (2012). For a new perspective on Italian philosophy since the Renaissance and Machiavelli's crucial place in it see Esposito (2012). The discussion of chance and providence in *The Prince* brings out Machiavelli's dialogue with Epicureanism and Platonism, respectively. For the latter, and in general on the relation between chance and God in the Florentine reception of Platonism, see Wind (1961) and Brown (1986). For Machiavelli's discussion of chance and his rejection of a theological narrative of history, see Pocock (1975) and Vatter (2000). On the relation between Machiavelli's theory of security and his views on chance and contingency, Dillon (2008) is illuminating. Nederman (2009b) and Viroli (2010) are recent attempts to take seriously Machiavelli's discourse on divine providence as being central to his political thought and not merely rhetorical adornment.

On the reception and influence of *The Prince* (Chapter Nine)

The contorted story of how *The Prince*, which remained unpublished and hardly read during Machiavelli's life, became the fundamental work of modern political thought has recently been told by Anglo (2005). The most discussed case study of Machiavelli's influence concerns the reception of his political ideas in the English revolutions: here compare the accounts of Pocock and Skinner with Rahe (2006 and 2009). For the study of Machiavelli's reception in the rest of Europe, see Procacci (1965 and 1995).

SELECTIVE
BIBLIOGRAPHY

Anglo, S. (2005), *Machiavelli – the First Century: Studies in Enthusiasm, Hostility and Irrelevance*, New York: Oxford University Press.

Althusser, L. (2011), *Machiavelli and Us*, London: Verso.

Aron, R. (1993), *Machiavel et les tyrannies modernes*, Paris: DeFallois.

Baron, H. (1988), *In Search of Florentine Civic Humanism: Essays on the Transition from Medieval to Modern Thought*. 2 vols, Princeton: Princeton University Press.

Barthas, J. (2012), *L'argent n'est pas le nerf de la guerre. Essai sur une prétendue erreur de Machiavel*, Rome, Collection de l'Ecole Française de Rome.

Bausi, F. (2005), *Machiavelli*, Roma: Salerno editore.

Bayona Aznar, B. (2007), "Marsilio de Padua y Maquiavelo: una lectura comparada", *Foro interno* (7), 11–34.

Berlin, I. (1980), "The Originality of Machiavelli", in *Against the Current. Essays in the History of Ideas*, New York: Penguin.

Black, R. (2010), "Machiavelli in the Chancery", in J. M. Najemy, *The Cambridge Companion to Machiavelli*, New York: Cambridge University Press.

Bracciolini, P. (1997), "In Praise of the Venetian Republic", in J. Kraye (ed.), *Cambridge Translations of Renaissance Philosophical Texts, vol. II. Political Philosophy*, Cambridge: Cambridge University Press.

Brown, A. (1986), "Platonism in Fifteenth-Century Florence and Its Contribution to Early Modern Thought", *Journal of Modern History* 58, 383–413.

—(1992), *The Medici in Florence. The Exercise and Language of Power*, Florence: Leo Olschki Editore.

—(2010), *The Return of Lucretius to Renaissance Florence*, Cambridge, MA: Harvard University Press.

Bruni, L. (1987), *Oration for the Funeral of Nanni Strozzi*, in G. Griffiths, J. Hankins, D. Thompson (eds), *The Humanism of Leonardo Bruni*, Binghamton: Medieval and Renaissance Texts and Studies.

Buber, M. (1964), *Königtum Gottes*, in M. Buber, *Werke. Zweiter Band. Schriften zur Bibel*, München: Koesel Verlag.

Burckhardt, J. (1958), *The Civilization of the Renaissance in Italy*, vol. I, New York: Harper & Row.

Butters, H. (2010), "Machiavelli and the Medici", in J. M. Najemy, *The Cambridge Companion to Machiavelli*, New York: Cambridge University Press.

Cassirer, E. (1963), *The Individual and the Cosmos in Renaissance Philosophy*, Philadelphia: University of Pennsylvania Press.

—(1974), *The Myth of the State*, New Haven: Yale University Press.

Chabod, F. (1958), *Machiavelli and the Renaissance*, Cambridge, MA: Harvard University Press.

Cicero (1991), *On Duties*, M. T. Griffith and E. M. Atkins (eds), Cambridge: Cambridge University Press.

Cutinelli-Rendina, Emanuele (1998), *Chiesa e religione in Machiavelli*, Pisa: Istituti editoriali e poligrafici.

—(1999), *Introduzione a Machiavelli*. Rome: Laterza.

Detienne, M. and Vernant, J.-P. (1974), *Les Ruses de l'Intelligence. La Métis des Grecs*, Paris: Flammarion.

Dillon, M. (2008), "Lethal Freedom," *Theory and Event* 11, 2.

Eliot, G. (1889), *Romola*, Florence: F. F. Lovell & Co.

Esposito, R. (2012), *Living Thought: The Origins and Actuality of Italian Philosophy*, Stanford: Stanford University Press.

Figgis, J. N. (1960), *Political Thought from Gerson to Grotius 1414–1625*, New York: Harper & Brothers.

Fontana, B. (1983), *Hegemony and Power. On the Relation Between Gramsci and Machiavelli*, Minneapolis: University of Minnesota Press.

Foucault, M. (2009), *Security, Territory, Population: Lectures at the Collège de France 1977–1978*, New York: Picador.

Fournel, J. L. and Zancarini J.C. (2002), "Machiavel: la guerre comme l'horizon de la politique", *Les cahiers de la Villa Gillet* 16, 137–57.

—(2003), *Les Guerres d'Italie: Des Batailles pour l'Europe (1494–1559)*, Paris: Gallimard.

Fubini, R. (1992), "From Social to Political Representation in Renaissance Florence", in K. R. A. Molho and J. Emlen (eds), *City States in Classical Antiquity and Medieval Italy*, Ann Arbor: University of Michigan Press.

Gaille-Nikodimov, M. (2004), *Conflit civil et liberté: la politique machiavélliene entre histoire et médicine*, Paris: Honoré Champion.

Geuna, M. (2005), "Machiavelli ed il ruolo dei conflitti nella vita politica", in D. Caruso and A. Arienzo (eds), *Conflitti*, Naples: Libreria Dante e Descartes.

—(2006), "Skinner, pre-humanist rhetorical culture and Machiavelli", in A. Brett and J. Tully (eds), *Rethinking the Foundations of Modern Political Thought*, Cambridge: Cambridge University Press.

Gilbert, F. (1939), "The Humanist Concept of the Prince and the Prince of Machiavelli", *The Journal of Modern History* 11(4), 449–83.

—(1949), "Bernardo Rucellai and the Orti Oricellari. A study on the Origin of Modern Political Thought", *Journal of the Warburg and Courtauld Institutes* 20, 187–214.

Ginzburg, C. (2003), "Machiavelli, l'eccezione e la regola. Linee di una ricerca in corso", *Quaderni storici* 112, 195–213.

—(2009), "Pontano, Machiavelli and Prudence: Some Further Reflections", in D. Ramada Curto, E. Dursteler, J. Kirshner, and F. Trivellano (eds), *From Florence to the Mediterreanean and Beyond. Essays in Honor of Anthony Molho*, Florence: Leo Olshki, 117–25.

Godman, P. (1998), *From Poliziano to Machiavelli: Florentine Humanism in the High Renaissance*, Princeton: Princeton University Press.

Greenblatt, S. (2011), *The Swerve. How the World Became Modern*, New York: W. W. Norton & Co.

Grossi, P. (2004), *L'ordine giuridico medievale*, Bari: Laterza.

Hankins, J. (ed.) (2000), *Renaissance Civic Humanism*, Cambridge: Cambridge University Press.

Hörnquist, M. (2004), *Machiavelli and Empire*, Cambridge: Cambridge University Press.

—(2010), "Machiavelli's military project and the *Art of War*", in J. M. Najemy, *The Cambridge Companion to Machiavelli*, New York: Cambridge University Press.

Inglese, G. (2006), *Per Machiavelli. L'arte dello stato, la cognizione delle storie*, Rome: Carocci editore.

Kahn, V. (1994), *Machiavellian Rhetoric from the Counter-Reformation to Milton*, Princeton: Princeton University Press.

—(2010), "Machiavelli's Afterlife and Reputation to the Eighteenth Century", in J. M. Najemy, *The Cambridge Companion to Machiavelli*, New York: Cambridge University Press.

Kantorowicz, E. (1997), *The King's Two Bodies: A Study in Medieval Political Theology*, Princeton: Princeton University Press.

Laclau, E. (2007), *On Populist Reason*, London: Verso.

Larivaille, P. (1982), *La Pensée politique de Machiavel*, Nancy: Presses Universitaires de Nancy.

—(2001), "Chapitre IX du Prince. La crise de la principauté civile", in Y. C. Zarka and T. Ménissier (eds), *Machiavel, le Prince ou le nouvel art politique*, Paris: PUF, 81–103

Lefort, C. (2012), *Machiavelli in the Making,* Evanston, IL: Northwestern University Press.

del Lucchese, F. (2011), *Conflict, Power and Multitude in Machiavelli and Spinoza*. London: Continuum.

Ludueña Romandini, F. (2006), *Homo oeconomicus. Marsilio Ficino, la teología y los misterios paganos*, Buenos Aires: Miño y Dávila.

Mansfield, H. (1996), *Machiavelli's Virtue*, Chicago: University of Chicago Press.

Martelli, M. (1982), "La logica provvidenzialistica e il capitolo 26 del Principe", *Interpres* 4, 262–384.

—(2009), *Otto studi machiavelliani*, Roma: Salerno editore

Marx, K. (1975), "On the Jewish Question", in K. Marx, *Early Writings*, New York: Vintage Books.

Masters, R. (1999), *Fortune is a River: Leonardo da Vinci and Niccolò Machiavelli's Magnificent Dream to Change the Course of Florentine History*, New York: Plume.

McCormick, J. (2011), *Machiavellian Democracy*, Cambridge: Cambridge University Press.

Meinecke, F. (1998), *Machiavellism: The Doctrine of Raison d'État and its Place in Modern History*, New Brunswick, NJ: Transaction Publishers.

Ménissier, T. (2001), "Chapitre premier du Prince", in Y. C. Zarka and T. Ménissier (eds), *Machiavel, le Prince ou le nouvel art politique*, Paris: PUF.

—(2010), *Machiavel ou la politique du centaure*, Paris: Éditions Hermann.

Morfino, V. (2006), "Tra Lucrezio e Spinoza: la Filosofia di Machiavelli", in F. del Lucchese, L. Sartorello, and S. Visentin (eds), *Machiavelli: Immaginazione e Contingenza*, Pisa: Edizioni ETS, 67–110.

Najemy, J. M. (2000), "Civil Humanism and Florentine Politics", in J. Hankins (ed.), *Renaissance Civic Humanism*, Cambridge: Cambridge University Press.

—(2010), *The Cambridge Companion to Machiavelli*, New York: Cambridge University Press.

Nederman, C. J. (2009a), *Lineages of European Political Thought: Explorations Along the Medieval/Modern Divide from John of Salisbury to Hegel*, Washington, DC: Catholic University of America Press.

—(2009b), *Machiavelli. A Beginner's Guide*, Oxford: Oneworld Publications.

Oakley, F. (2006), *Kingship: The Politics of Enchantment*, Oxford: Blackwell.

Pesman, R. (2010), "Machiavelli, Piero Soderini, and the republic of 1494–1512", in J. M. Najemy, *The Cambridge Companion to Machiavelli*, New York: Cambridge University Press.

Pettit, P. (1999), *Republicanism. A Theory of Freedom and Government*, Cambridge: Cambridge University Press.

Pitkin, H. (1967), *The Concept of Representation*, Berkeley: University of California Press.

Plato (1980), *The Laws*, Thomas Pangle (trans.), New York: Basic Books.

Pocock, J. (1975), *The Machiavellian Moment*, Princeton: Princeton University Press.

Procacci, G. (1965), *Studi sulla fortuna del Machiavelli*, Rome: Istituto Storico Italiano.

—(1995), *Machiavelli nella cultura europea dell'età moderna*, Bari: Laterza.

Rahe, P. (2000), "Situating Machiavelli", in J. Hankins, *Renaissance Civic Humanism*, Cambridge: Cambridge University Press, 270–308.

—(2007), "In the Shadow of Lucretius: The Epicurean Foundations of Machiavelli's Political Thought", *History of Political Thought* 28(1), 30–55.

—(2009), *Against Throne and Altar. Machiavelli and Political Theory under the English Republic*, Cambridge: Cambridge University Press.

Rahe, P. (ed.) (2006), *Machiavelli's Liberal Republican Legacy*, Cambridge: Cambridge University Press.

Rubinstein, N. (2004), *Studies in Italian History in the Middle Ages and the Renaissance*. Vol. 1, Rome: Edizioni di Storia e Letteratura.

Ruiz Stull, M. (2009), "La política de *De Rerum Natura*. Efectos del *clinamen* en la idea de comunidad de Lucrecio", *Atenea 500*, 42–54.

Santoro, M. (1966), *Fortuna, ragione e prudenza nella civiltà letteraria del Cinquecento*, Naples: Liguori.

Saralegui, M. (2012), *Maquiavelo y la contradicción. Un estudio sobre fortuna, virtud y la teoría del acción*, Pamplona: Ediciones Universidad de Navarra.

Sasso, G. (1987–8), *Machiavelli e gli antichi e altri saggi*, 3 vols, Milan–Naples: Ricciardi editore.

—(1993), *Niccolò Machiavelli*, 2 vols, Bologna: Il Mulino.

Silk, M. (2004), "Numa Pompilius and the Idea of Civil Religion in the West", *Journal of the American Academy of Religion*, 72(4), 863–96.

Skinner, Q. (1978), *The Foundations of Modern Political Thought*, 2 vols, Cambridge: Cambridge University Press.

—(1981), *Machiavelli. A Very Short Introduction*, Oxford: Oxford University Press.

—(2002), *Visions of Politics. Volume 2: Renaissance Virtues*, Cambridge: Cambridge University Press.

—(2009), "A Genealogy of the Modern State", *Proceedings of the British Academy* 162, 325–70.

Spinoza, B. (2007), *Theological-Political Treatise*, Cambridge: Cambridge University Press.

Springborg, P. (1992), *Western Republicanism and the Oriental Prince*, Austin: University of Texas Press.

Stacey, P. (2007), *Roman Monarchy and the Renaissance Prince*, New York: Cambridge University Press.

Stephens, J. N. (1988), "Ciceronian Rhetoric and the Immorality of Machiavelli's Prince", *Renaissance Studies* II, 258–67.

Strauss, L. (1957), "Machiavelli's Intention: The Prince", *American Political Science Review*, 51(1), 13–40.

—(1958), *Thoughts on Machiavelli*, Chicago: University of Chicago Press.

—(2000), *On Tyranny*, Chicago: University of Chicago Press.

Sullivan, V. B. (1996), *Machiavelli's Three Romes: Religion, Human Liberty, and Politics Reformed*, DeKalb, IL: Northern Illinois University Press.

—(2004), *Machiavelli, Hobbes, and the Formation of a Liberal Republicanism in England*, Cambridge: Cambridge University Press.

Syros, V. (2011), "Founders and Kings versus Orators: Medieval and Early Modern Views on the Origin of Social Life", *Viator* 42(1), 383–408.

—(2012), "Indian Emergencies: Baranī's *Fatāwā-i Jahāndārī*, the Diseases of the Body Politic, and Machiavelli's *accidenti*", *Philosophy East & West* 62(4), 545–73.

Vatter, M. (2000), *Between Form and Event. Machiavelli's Theory of Political Freedom*, Dordrecht: Kluwer Academic Publishers.

Viroli, M. (1998), *Il sorriso di Machiavelli. Storia di Machiavelli*, Bari: Laterza.

—(2005), *From Politics to Reason of State: the Acquisition and Transformation of the Language of Politics 1250–1600*, Cambridge: Cambridge University Press.

—(2010), *Machiavelli's God*, Princeton: Princeton University Press.

Voegelin, E. (1952), *The New Science of Politics*, Chicago: The University of Chicago Press.

Vuillemin, J. (1984), *Nécessité ou contingence. L'aporie de Diodore et les systèmes philosophiques*, Paris: Les Editions de Minuit.

Warburg, A. (1996), *La rinascita del paganesimo antico*, Florence: La Nuova Italia.

Wind, E. (1961), "Platonic tyranny and Renaissance Fortuna: on Ficino's reading of *Laws*, IV, 709a–712b", in M. Meiss (ed.), *Essays in honor of Erwin Panofsky*, New York: New York University Press.

Zarka, Y. C. and Ménissier, T. (eds.) (2001), *Machiavel, le Prince ou le nouvel art politique*, Paris: PUF.

INDEX OF NAMES

INDEX